The Music Makers Approach:
inclusive activities for young children with special educational needs

by

Hannah Mortimer

Irene – With best wishes and happy music making

Hannah

NASEN

A NASEN Publication

Published in 2000

© Hannah Mortimer

All rights reserved. With the exception of pages 70 to 75, no part of this publication may be reproduced or transmitted in any form or by any means, electronic, mechanical, photocopying, recording, or otherwise, without the prior permission of the publishers.

ISBN 1 901 485 22 6

The right of the author to be identified as author of this work has been asserted by her in accordance with the Copyright, Designs and Patents Act 1988.

NASEN

Published by NASEN.
NASEN is a registered charity. Charity No. 1007023.
NASEN is a company limited by guarantee, registered in England and Wales.
Company No. 2674379.

Further copies of this book and details of NASEN's many other publications may be obtained from the NASEN Bookshop at its registered office:

NASEN House, 4/5 Amber Business Village, Amber Close, Tamworth, Staffs. B77 4RP.
Tel: 01827 311500. Fax: 01827 313005. Email: welcome@nasen.org.uk
Web site: www.nasen.org.uk

Cover design by Raphael Creative Design.
Typeset by Jenny Shelley.
Typeset in Times and printed in the United Kingdom by Stowes (Stoke-on-Trent).

The Music Makers Approach
Contents

	Page
Introduction	**6**
Why music?	6
Inclusive education	6
The Music Makers project	6
Requirements of the Code of Practice for SEN	7
The Early Learning Goals	7
Different settings	7
Involving parents	8
Keeping records	8
How to use this book	8
Chapter 1: Welcoming a child with special educational needs to the group	**9**
Contacting the parents	9
Gathering information	10
A model for assessment and record-keeping	10
The Code of Practice for SEN	10
How to use the activities to plan approaches for meeting SEN	11
Liaising with other professionals	11
Step-by-step teaching	12
Use of praise and encouragement	13
Partnership with parents	13
Providing outreach support and a warm welcome	13
Chapter 2: Meeting the Early Learning Goals	**14**
Meeting all the children's needs inclusively	14
How your music session can contribute towards each Early Learning Goal	14
Preparing for inspection; evidence of planning	14
Adapting the approach for older children	15
Chapter 3: Getting ready for music	**16**
What you will need	16
How to organise your music session	16
Holding their attention; balance and flow	17
Purchasing or making your own instruments; what to collect	18
Chapter 4: Enjoying music together	**19**
Activity 4.1: Warming Up	19
Activity 4.2: Greeting Song	20
Activity 4.3: Old Macdonald's Makaton Farm	21
Activity 4.4: The Shaking Game	22
Activity 4.5: Jelly on a Plate	23
Activity 4.6: Everybody Clap Hands	24
Activity 4.7: It's Time to Say 'Goodbye'	25
Activity 4.8: Alternative Goodbye song	26

The Music Makers Approach

	Page
Chapter 5: Songs and action rhymes	**27**
Activity 5.1: The Monster Stomp	27
Activity 5.2: Everybody Copy Me	28
Activity 5.3: Benjie Hammers with One Hammer	29
Activity 5.4: Row, Row, Row Your Boat	30
Activity 5.5: Incy Wincy Spider	31
Activity 5.6: The Grand Old Duke of York	32
Activity 5.7: Jack-in-the-Box	33
Activity 5.8: The Wheels on the Bus	34
Chapter 6: Looking and listening games	**35**
Activity 6.1: Find the Sound	35
Activity 6.2: The Pointing Game	36
Activity 6.3: Feely Bag	37
Activity 6.4: A Listening Walk	38
Activity 6.5: The Dinosaur Hunt	39
Activity 6.6: Hunt the Mouse	40
Activity 6.7: Swanee Whistles	41
Activity 6.8: Pass the Sound	42
Chapter 7: Movement and rhythm games	**43**
Activity 7.1: Drum Beats	43
Activity 7.2: Cobbler, Cobbler	44
Activity 7.3: Musical Bumps and Old Favourites	45
Activity 7.4: The Kangaroo Song	46
Activity 7.5: Five Little Speckled Frogs	47
Activity 7.6: Heads, Shoulders, Knees and Toes	48
Activity 7.7: The Crocodile Song	49
Activity 7.8: Dinner on the Train	50
Chapter 8: Concepts and understanding	**51**
Activity 8.1: Favourite Colours	51
Activity 8.2: Four Currant Buns	52
Activity 8.3: Nose, Nose, Show Me Your Nose	53
Activity 8.4: Goldilocks	54
Activity 8.5: This Is the Way	55
Activity 8.6: Musical Positions	56
Activity 8.7: The Music Man	57
Activity 8.8: This Old Man	58
Chapter 9: Band time	**59**
Activity 9.1: Join the Band	59
Activity 9.2: Loudly and Quietly	60
Activity 9.3: Runaway Train	61

	Page
Activity 9.4: Musical Swaps	62
Activity 9.5: Leading the Band	63
Activity 9.6: Musical Stories	64
Activity 9.7: Watch the Conductor	65
Activity 9.8: Marching	66

Chapter 10: Snapshot of the Music Makers Approach in action — 67

Chapter 11: The evaluative research — 68

Early Learning Goals: Reference numbers used in activity sheets — 70

Photocopiable assessment and record-keeping sheets — 73
- Music Makers: Assessment and record-keeping sheet — 73
- Music Makers: Session planning sheet — 75

Resource list and references — 76

Acknowledgements

Dedicated to the young music makers of Hambleton and Richmondshire.

With acknowledgements to the North Yorkshire Joint Funding Small Innovative Projects grant for making the development of these materials possible, and to the North Yorkshire Pupil and Parent Services and the Northallerton NHS Trust for releasing me for the project.

Every effort has been made to trace the ownership of all copyrighted material and to secure the necessary permissions to reprint any of these words. In the event of any questions arising as to the use of any material, the author and the publisher, while expressing regret for any inadvertent error, will be happy to make the necessary correction in any future printings.

This publication includes images from Art Today, Dover Books and Corel PrintHouse. Used under licence.

Introduction

Why music?

Music is an amazing thing. It stills a crying baby. It captures a toddler's attention. It holds the interest of children who, in any other situation, might be experiencing considerable learning or communication difficulties. It provides opportunities for even very young children to join together sociably in a group, long before they are old enough to attend an early years setting. It encourages children who find it hard to move, to move more freely. It encourages children who do not like to look and to listen to do just that. And, above all, it is fun.

As such a powerful tool, it is not surprising that music can be used very effectively to teach young children to learn and to develop. In this book, you will be helped to develop a regular music session as part of your early learning activities. Not only will this become a useful way of working towards the Early Learning Goals for the foundation stage of learning, but you can use it to welcome and include children with a wide range of special needs. You can also adapt the activities if you are working with older children, or if you are planning your sessions within a special school.

Inclusive education

You may have heard a great deal over the past 20 years about integrating children with special needs into mainstream settings. This musical approach takes the idea much further. It encourages you to provide *inclusive* activities which suit *all* your children, regardless of need. Therefore the activities should be flexible enough both to match admirably the needs of your older children as they prepare for starting school, and also of all children on the special educational needs register. It is a little like adapting a classroom. During *integration*, you provide a platform to raise the child in the wheelchair to a height where she can see out of the window. In *inclusive* education, you simply adapt all of the windows so that everybody has a clear view.

The Music Makers project

Several years ago, I started a regular developmental music group at a child development centre as part of the multidisciplinary service for pre-school children with special needs. Parents joined us from all around with the excellent support of the voluntary transport service. These sessions were much enjoyed by the children, but also became a useful way of teaching them new developmental milestones, using music as the attention-getter and motivator. This makes the sessions rather different from *music therapy* where children are encouraged to respond and express themselves through the therapeutic medium of music. In *developmental music therapy*, music simply becomes the tool used to teach developmental steps.

We asked the parents and therapists already working with the children to provide us with an idea of what each child could do, and to mark particular targets they would like the child to achieve through attending the group. This is a similar approach to the one you will read about in Chapter 1, and the assessment we used is similar to that you will be using on page 73. We were delighted with how the children responded, and the parents were keen to see the groups continue. However, for some of them, it was a long way to travel with a small child.

Introduction

In April 1997, we were successful in obtaining a grant through a Joint Finance Small Innovative Projects initiative. This money allowed us to continue our child development centre group, and also to provide satellite groups around the area. It has also enabled many pre-school playgroups to become trained in the approaches so that, week by week, they could take over the running of a group and welcome any local children with special needs who were able to join them. I was also able to give additional voluntary time to collecting the materials and approaches together in a book to support those early years educators taking part in the project. This book is the result.

Requirements of the Code of Practice for SEN

Pre-schools need to have regard to the *Code of Practice on the Identification and Assessment of Special Educational Needs* (DfE, 1994), and this book suggests one approach for designing individual education plans to suit children on the special needs register. The procedure is explained in simple and practical terms, again using musical activities as a vehicle for teaching your targets, but with suggestions for helping the children generalise the skills learned into the rest of their play.

You will be helped to share your approaches with the family, and you will also be led through a form of assessment and record-keeping which you can use to gather baseline information, set targets and record progress. There are also suggestions for liaising with other professionals who might be involved. All this you will find in Chapter 1.

The Early Learning Goals

Because the activities suggested are designed to be inclusive for all children, you will be able to use them to plan learning outcomes for children working towards the Early Learning Goals. Each activity is cross-referenced to the Early Learning Goal it contributes towards, and the key used is given on page 70. You will be helped to plan your activities and to provide evidence of your planning ready for OFSTED inspection. You will also be helped to adapt each activity flexibly to suit your older children and also those who might need additional help or a less challenging approach.

Different settings

You are likely to be doing your musical activities in a whole range of different settings. Some of you might be starting a regular music slot as part of your existing early years session. Some of you might be in nursery classes or schools, some in assessment nurseries or special schools, some in Social Services family centres, some in parent and toddler groups, some in health centres. We have used the approach in all of these settings, including in groups for parents and toddlers where there are particular challenges in managing the children's behaviour. In this case, the activities provided a useful tool for encouraging the children to join in co-operatively in a group, to look and listen for instructions, and, above all, to share fun and pleasure with the adults in their lives.

There is nothing new or specialist about the activities. Each one should feel utterly familiar and practicable. This book helps you use these very familiar activities in a structured and planned way, and to maintain important evidence that you are setting out to meet special educational needs and to work towards the Early Learning Goals.

The Music Makers Approach

Involving parents

It is likely that the parents who come to your group will have been sharing musical moments with their children long before your musical activities were begun. Research is now telling us just how important early lap play and nursery songs and rhymes are to the developing child's two-way communication, language, and even later reading skills. Do involve parents fully. This book will share ideas for involving parents and families in the music groups and extending the activities to home.

Make a special welcome to parents in your neighbourhood who might have a young child with special educational needs. It does not matter if they do not belong to your setting. Why not tell your health visitor that you are starting a developmental music group and that you would welcome young visitors with special needs who might benefit? Local families could then join your session for the half-hour music group, and have the opportunity to get to know other parents in their area.

It does not matter about the child's age either. These activities have been successfully used in groups of mixed age pre-school children from babyhood to rising five and beyond. Why not invite parents and younger siblings to join the session once you are confident, and use it as a useful introduction to pre-school for your future customers?

Keeping records

In these times of accountability, you are becoming increasingly used to keeping records; records of your activities, records of your planning, records of your individual assessments, records of progress and 'added value'. The assessment and record-keeping sheets on page 73 will come as no surprise but, in order to be useful, need to fit in with what you are already required to do. That is why each activity is linked to both the Early Learning Goals and to the assessment target for the child with special needs. Hopefully, this cross-referencing will be a useful aid as you prepare your record-keeping both for inspection and for meeting the requirements of the *Code of Practice* for SEN.

How to use this book

When we trained colleagues in the project, they were introduced to the chapters stage by stage in order to become gradually familiar with the approach, and to plan more and more of the music sessions themselves without the trainer's help. This 'step-by-small-step' approach is already familiar to those of you who are used to developmental teaching. If you are planning a developmental music group, start small and gradually build up your activities as you become more confident. You will find a session planning sheet on page 75 to help you. You will find the activities collected in Chapters 4 to 9 will fit with the sections on the session planning sheet. This will enable you to plan a balanced session, and also to include activities to meet particular needs or cover particular Early Learning Goals.

You will not need to be proficient on a musical instrument, as a cassette recorder and tapes can be used instead. Others of you might like to revive old skills on a guitar or keyboard, and you will find the resource list on page 76 helpful. All of you need to practise your singing. It is only by doing it that it gets better. Even if you sing out of tune, learn to do it with confidence and style! It is your enthusiasm rather than your proficiency which will encourage the children to join in. And singing does improve the more you do it. Good luck!

Chapter 1
Welcoming a child with special educational needs to the group

In this chapter, we look at how you can include young children with special educational needs into your regular music sessions, how to plan for their needs, and how to have regard to the Code of Practice for SEN.

Contacting the parents

Let us suppose that you work in an early years setting. Once you have decided to hold a regular Music Makers session, you will want to ensure that you have contacted all the parents of children in your area who might benefit. Where do you start?

You will need to approach this sensitively. Sadly, the very act of categorising children as 'having special needs' can segregate the needs of these children from those of the rest of the population in people's minds. Think back to your definition of 'inclusive' activities on page 6, and make sure that *your* sessions are available to all children, regardless of need.

Your health visitor might be the best first contact. Ask her or him to help you make sure you have invited any children to the group who might benefit. Perhaps there are children who, by nature of their development, do not attend their local early years setting but attend a child development centre or a part-time special nursery instead. Perhaps there are children who are living in temporary foster care who would benefit from joining the group for sessions with their foster carer. Perhaps there are children whose behaviour has been challenging outside the home, but who might find it easy to behave during a half-hour's highly motivating music group. In other words, do consider inviting children to join just the music session, even if they are not a member of your local group.

In the Music Makers project, we wrote to parents of all children attending the local child development centre who were two, three or four years old. We asked them firstly if their child already attended a local pre-school group and whether that group would appreciate training in the setting up of a developmental music group. This book covers the training they received. Secondly we asked them whether they would like to join their local pre-school just for the half hour of the music session. We then matched families up to local groups willing to include them and willing to train in the approach.

Parents were always invited to be with their child during the sessions, sharing the fun and supporting their learning. We learned not to ask parents of older or school-age children to attend as a matter of course, since some felt that the sessions were an opportunity for their child to learn how to join in fully without them being present. However, the invitation to choose was always made.

Many other parents chose to join us also, and it was helpful to have an adult-child ratio for the whole group of at least four children to one adult. In a 'behaviour group' which we ran in conjunction with the local health visitors, we were delighted to welcome fathers and mothers together, the working partner managing to arrange to be with us in order to share some of the enjoyment of seeing their child learn and behave in a group with other children.

The Music Makers Approach

Gathering information

Before you begin to plan activities to meet any particular special needs, you will need to know what skills the child who has special needs already has, and decide what your targets should be. This assessment and target setting will provide the information you need to plan an individual education programme for that child, along the guidelines of the *Code of Practice*. This will be explained later. The assessment sheet which we developed in the Music Makers project is shown on page 73. We used this assessment in three ways.

Firstly, we gave a copy to the parents of the child with special needs, as a way of showing the curriculum of activities we would be following, but also asking them to let us know what the child could do at present, and what skills the parents would realistically like their child to learn in music group over the next term. They were invited to enter one tick in the initial assessment column if the child could sometimes do that skill, and two ticks if they could do it reliably in many different situations. This enabled us to select those skills which were perhaps 'emerging' for the child and build on those first for a successful start. In planning 'next steps' for each child, we selected the skill that was only a little more challenging than the skill before, teaching step by very small step. Sometimes we found it necessary to break the steps down even smaller than those on the assessment sheet when we were teaching.

We also used the assessment form to send to other professionals already working with the child. These included physiotherapists, speech and language therapists, pre-school teachers, teachers at specialist nurseries, psychologists and health visitors. This enabled the whole team of professionals working with the child to contribute to the assessment and planning for that child. Thirdly, we added our own observations of how the child responded during the first session or two.

When we had received the replies, we were able to combine these together into a planned programme of activities for that child, and to return a term later to assess progress. On this occasion, we used our own observations of how the child responded in the group, and kept parents and professionals involved with the results of our teaching.

A model for assessment and record-keeping

You will see that the assessment sheet is broken down into certain areas which relate, more or less, to the sections on the session planning sheet on page 75. These skills correspond to developmental stages from approximately six months to four years and, though in no particular order, are roughly ranked from easiest skill to most challenging within any one activity area.

The Code of Practice for SEN

Your group is likely to find itself using these musical special needs approaches because you have a child or children whose names have been placed on the setting's special educational needs register. Perhaps you have a child attending who you already know has special educational needs. You may have been approached by parents, health visitor, social worker, or early years support teacher and asked whether you could provide a part-time place for the child. In this case, you will need to gather information about who is already involved and use parents very much as experts on their own child to plan your approaches.

1. Welcoming a child with special educational needs to the group

It could also be that you are identifying a special need for the first time within the group. Perhaps, even after a settling-in time, you have a child who is very insecure within the group, a child who appears to be playing at a very immature level, a child who finds eye contact and social interaction particularly difficult, or a child whose behaviour does not respond to your usual methods and approaches. It will be helpful if you understand the graduated approach given in the revised *Code of Practice*.

If you feel that you will need to adapt your approaches significantly in order to meet the needs of an individual child whose progress, behaviour or emotional state concerns you, then you will need to keep a special record of the action you take, keeping parents closely in touch as you follow a graduated approach for assessing what the child needs to learn next, planning how you are going to teach it, and who is going to be involved. About one-fifth of all children might experience SEN at some stage of their school lives.

Once a child's progress is being clearly monitored, you will need to adapt your approaches within the group to cater for that child, negotiating your approaches with parents and meeting at least termly to review progress. If the child seems to need additional action from within your setting, you will need to produce an individual education plan for the child, targeting particular learning outcomes and planning who is going to teach them, and how. Again, this needs to be shared and negotiated with parents. In most early years settings, this will be put together with help from the setting's special needs co-ordinator or 'SENCO'.

Children who continue to experience special educational needs despite this intervention may need assessment and guidance from outside professionals. You will find it helpful to talk with the local health visitor, early years advisory teacher or educational psychologist for advice on referral. Sometimes, you might need general advice on approaches for managing challenging behaviour, or for encouraging a child with autistic difficulties to join into a group. A very few children may go on to receive statutory assessment and perhaps a Statement of Special Educational Needs which involves support and sometimes additional resources from the local education authority (LEA).

In your individual education plan, you will need to record the nature of the child's difficulty, the action you will take, what help the parents will provide, your targets for this term, and when you will be holding a review meeting with the parents. You will find an example on the next page.

How to use the activities to plan approaches for meeting SEN

Once you have combined all your initial assessment forms from parents, yourselves and other professionals, you will be able to select target skills to include in your education plan for that child. First look at skills which the child can do sometimes but not always. Then move on to the next most difficult skill. Look for opportunities for generalising each skill into the rest of the play session, using the ideas in the activity Chapters 4 to 9.

Liaising with other professionals

If you have been monitoring a child's needs within your setting under the *Code of Practice* for a term or two, and you are still concerned that progress is not being made, then you might wish to talk to parents and see if they would agree to a referral to one of the outside professional agencies.

The Music Makers Approach

Again, the health visitor might prove a useful link between group and home if you are not sure of your ground or your reception. At other times, the parents themselves will be concerned and anxious for help and might wish to refer themselves, either through a clinic doctor, a health visitor, or direct to the Education Support Service at your local education offices. Once an outside agency is involved, they should be able to help you plan for the child and to monitor their progress. You will need to take on board the professional recommendations in setting the individual education plan.

Individual Education Plan

Name: Holly Smith
Stage: 2
Nature of difficulty: Holly's development is still immature and is about a year behind her age, according to the health visitor.

Action
1. Elaine will ask the health visitor for further information and find out if another professionals are involved.
2. Vicky and Sue will observe Holly over two music sessions and complete the initial assessment form.
3. Select activities for a regular music group which encourage Holly to look and to listen in the group and to copy actions.
4. Follow up these activities in the rest of the session; Elaine will work alongside Holly for part of each day.
5. Find out about training; Sue will find out about possible 'Portage' training next summer.

Help from parents: John and Carrie will also fill in the initial assessment form, and Carrie will come in for music so that she can extend the activities at home.

Targets for this term
1. Holly will look and listen to the music leader during each activity.
2. Holly will join in the keywords in a familiar action song.
3. Holly will begin to imitate simple actions, such as clapping and waving.
4. Holly will begin to play more constructively with the toys and playthings.

Review meeting with parents: July 18th after morning session. Invite health visitor.

Step-by-step teaching

For children with significant and long-term special educational needs, you might find that steps need to be broken down very finely in order for the child to learn and to develop. Learning only takes place with success, so it is vital to plan activities at just the right level for the child to feel successful. Your praise and encouragement will make all the difference to this.

1. Welcoming a child with special educational needs to the group

Use of praise and encouragement

One of the advantages of the musical approach is that it brings with it its own motivation and enjoyment. When you are involving a child with special needs in your group, you will need to ensure that an adult sits alongside, models all the actions, prompts the child to respond (with physical help if necessary) and makes the whole process fun and enjoyable. Your smiles, your constant praise and your enthusiasm will all be key elements to success. You can pick out any of the children by name to praise certain behaviours: '*William*'s looking', 'Mary, you're watching me *beautifully*', 'Philip, you *are* marching well today'.

In responding to your children, you need to be always 'on your toes', ready to change the activity flexibly, ready to vary the pace, ready to swoop into band time if they are losing interest. I used to tell the parents not to worry about their child's behaviour in the group; if they did not concentrate, it would be my fault for not keeping it interesting enough! That is both the challenge and the amazing effect of running a music group.

Partnership with parents

You are required to keep parents and carers closely in touch with all your planning and intervention for children with special needs. This partnership and ongoing communication will work best if you share the good news as well as the bad right from the start. You will find it difficult to establish trust between you if you adopt this attitude: 'Let's wait and see; we don't want to worry the parents until we know that something is really *wrong*.' Instead, you need to be planning and monitoring the children's progress and challenges all of the time, so that your special needs assessment and record-keeping arise naturally out of what you are doing day to day.

Providing outreach support and a warm welcome

Once you are running your music group with confidence, why not invite in other children and parents who would benefit? You could also provide a newsletter to keep all your parents in touch with your musical activities, with particular reference to follow-up activities at home. Why not open your doors to other early years or special needs colleagues in the locality to show them one practical way of meeting special needs and of including all children flexibly in your activities?

Chapter 2
Meeting the Early Learning Goals

Meeting all the children's needs inclusively

You will already be familiar with the planning and record-keeping required under the Early Learning Goals (QCA and DfEE, 2000), including the preparation for inspection. Much of your planning for individual children with special educational needs should overlap with the planning you are doing of your curriculum, your short, medium and long-term plans of activities, and your individual assessment of each child within your group.

Through your planning, you can ensure that you have covered all aspects of the curriculum, that you have allowed each child to join in all the activities, that you have involved all your staff and that you have information to share with parents so that they can support the activities at home.

You need to keep evidence that your whole curriculum is balanced and that most children are likely to achieve the Early Learning Goals by the time they finish the foundation stage. These Early Learning Goals are listed on page 70, and given a reference number which is cross-referenced to the activity pages to help you with this planning.

You should aim to make all your activities inclusive for children with special educational needs; they have joined your group to be a part of it and should be following the same curriculum, albeit at a level appropriate to their ability. You will need to look carefully at the child's strengths, needs and interests when planning how to include them in each activity. Though you might use strategies suitable for younger children to help children who are less mature in their development, take care to use songs, instruments and resources suitable to their actual age. A child of four who is learning similar skills to a two-and-a-half-year-old is likely to develop low self-esteem if always provided with much younger rhymes and activities.

How your music session can contribute towards each Early Learning Goal

If you look at each of the activity pages in Chapters 4 to 9, you will see a list of the Early Learning Goals towards which that activity contributes. This will be useful evidence when showing how you are planning to cover all the goals, and how you are striving to provide a balanced curriculum. The areas of personal, social and emotional development and creative development figure largely, but you will also see how music can be usefully adopted to teach learning goals from the areas of language and literacy, mathematics, knowledge and understanding of the world, and physical development.

You can, of course, adapt the approach for older children and integrate the planning of your activities with the National Curriculum. The author has found that most of the activities adapt well for older children. They can also be extended for able children by allowing them a greater say in the session and encouraging them to lead and initiate ideas as well as to join in and to follow.

Preparing for inspection; evidence of planning

If your early years setting is subject to inspection, you may choose to hold your music making session as usual. Whilst it is unlikely that every area of learning will be covered in one session, the inspector will be able to look at your curriculum plans and record-keeping and see how you are using your music sessions to cover all areas of learning. You should keep other useful evidence of your planning, including examples of the children's musical activities, and any photographic or video recording too.

Your planning should also show that you have a range of activities which contribute to your curriculum. Some should be in small groups, some in larger, but you should also plan opportunities for children to play independently, depending on the particular activity. Each activity should relate to a particular learning goal and to the numbers, ages and stages of the children involved. The activity chapters in this book follow this requirement and show how this can be done in practice.

Nursery inspectors have been given a very precise 'Inspection Framework' to follow. They will be looking at four aspects of the educational provision your group provides. Firstly, they will be inspecting the planning and content of your educational programme and how well it contributes to children's attainments and progress in the area of personal and social development. Then they will look at the quality of your teaching, including the methods you use, your knowledge of each child's abilities, and your expectations of their progress. Thirdly, they will look at the way in which you assess your children's attainments and progress. Finally, the inspectors will look at the effectiveness of your partnership between parents and early years carers.

Your session planning sheets, showing which activities you have used, and towards which special needs targets and Early Learning Goals they contribute, will provide useful evidence of your planning and teaching at inspection time.

Adapting the approach for older children

Although the activities in this book are all linked to different Early Learning Goals, most will also be of benefit to older children working within the National Curriculum framework. The author has used these activities with KS1 children in mainstream settings and has also found them easy to adapt for older primary classes in special schools. The children's interest and motivation will tell you whether you have planned the level correctly.

Chapter 3
Getting ready for music

What you will need

When you decide to start a music group, you will need to start collecting musical instruments, and you will find suggestions for these below. You can usefully build this into a project on music or sound, helping the children to make a range of percussive and shaking instruments.

You will also need some musical accompaniment. Perhaps you can harness some local musical talent and encourage a neighbour, fellow teacher or parent to play the piano or guitar for you, or fund-raise for an electronic keyboard. If not, a cassette recorder and tapes can work well. Make sure the quality of sound is good, and have one adult on standby to manage the machine so that the group leader does not need to worry about it. You will need to take time before the session to ensure all the tapes are the right way round and at the correct place.

Choose tapes and accompaniments which are simple and not drowned out with too much background sound and jazzy harmonics; the children need to hear the tune line. Look for tapes and soundtracks which represent all the richness of our multicultural society. You might be able to record a pianist playing, or ask someone with a strong voice to put the favourite songs on tape for you. Some of the activities suggest particular tunes and tapes which you might find useful. Look on page 76 for resource suggestions.

You will also need a suitable area of the premises or hall to hold the group in. A large hall is fine so long as you use carpet squares to signal to the children where to plant themselves, and arrange them in a circle facing the leader. The leader should sit at the end of the circle nearest the wall so that the children are facing away from the attraction of the large space in the remainder of the hall. This way, they are less inclined to run around. Alternatively, you can have a circle of chairs for adults around the edge, and a 'song carpet' in the centre of the ring for the children to sit on.

We have held other groups successfully on the story mat of a playroom or class. The idea is to define the boundary clearly (a mat or a chair shows the children just where to sit) and to have all the children and adults able both to face each other and the leader; hence the idea of the circle. Young children and some of those who have special needs may well wish or need to sit next to a parent or adult, or on a parent's knee. In the groups we hold in child development centres, we all sit on the floor in a large circle; parents, children, siblings, therapists, leader and all.

How to organise your music session

Use the session planning sheet on page 75 to help you plan the activities, aiming for 20 minutes to half an hour's duration.

First choose a well-known favourite to signal the beginning of a session and become your theme tune. 'If you're happy and you know it' involves actions and familiar words, is easy to pick up, and seems to be liked by most of the children. Other favourites could be 'The wheels on the bus' or 'The music man' (*Okki-tokki-unga*). This should be your warm-up song at the beginning of every session; stay with the favourite and only consider changing every term or so if you really need to. The warm-up song both lets the children know that music is about to begin, makes them feel secure with its familiarity, and immediately gives them an action to do to get going.

3. Getting ready for music

You then need a greeting song to include and welcome all your children into music time. Make sure to include the names of any visiting siblings, toddlers or babies. You should greet each child with a name, a look and a smile, perhaps a wave too. Ideally, you should encourage the children to look at you as you sing, and respond with a smile or a wave. You should also encourage every single adult to join in the singing of this greeting song and you will find the older children join in too. Never expect all the children to join in singing all the songs. Both singing and doing actions at the same time are difficult for pre-school children, but are much more likely if the adults are doing it too. You will find activities suitable for warm-ups and greetings in Chapter 4.

Next move on to a couple of action rhymes. You will find ideas for these in Chapter 5 and many more in the books listed on the resources page at the end of this book. Keep the actions simple, starting with only one or two verses and building up until the children are familiar with the songs. Always try to have one well-known action rhyme and only introduce one new rhyme in any one session. Make sure all the adults model the actions, especially if you yourself are reading unfamiliar words or playing an accompaniment. Some of the younger or less mature children might be helped by a hand-over-hand prompt. Take the songs slowly to give the children time to respond.

Now turn to Chapter 6 for ideas for looking and listening games. Take the chance throughout all the activities to praise good looking and listening, naming the children who are succeeding and trying to name all of them at some point. Movement activities are included in Chapter 7. This has been placed near the end of the session since, once mobile, the children's initial attention and concentration might be lessened. Think ahead about the space you might need for this activity, and choose activities accordingly.

Whilst you come back to the circle and rest from your movement, a spoken rhyme will provide a useful remission. Choose activities from Chapter 8. Finally (and sooner if you find attention waning; you will find you can stretch the music session to half an hour once you become more confident and fluent) choose activities from the band time, Chapter 9. Bring in the box of musical instruments which should have been hidden out of sight for the first part of the session. Allow the children to choose their own instruments, allowing non-ambulant children time to crawl, bottom-shuffle or be lifted to the box in order to take part in the choosing. I usually start with the simple activity 9.1, and then include two or three other band time activities, finishing with the grand march in activity 9.8.

Always finish with the same 'goodbye' song, again naming each child and encouraging a look, a smile or a wave. You will find suggestions for this also in Chapter 4.

Holding their attention; balance and flow

The pattern of the sessions has been designed to vary the pace and flow between action, song, looking and listening, speech, movement and instrument play. The children might quickly lose interest if you sat and sang songs for a full half hour. By varying the presentation in this way, you will find you can hold attention for 15 minutes or so when you first get going, gradually building up to 30 minutes. Do not attempt longer at this age and stage.

Use your own movements (approaching the children close, or moving between them) to hold eyes and attention. Keep one or two surprises up your sleeve to renew interest. Use 'props' to look at and to hold in order to catch their interest. Use their names and your praise to hold attention.

The Music Makers Approach

Keep children with a short attention span next to an adult who can help to focus their watching and demonstrate what to do to them directly. Try to keep this fun and non-confrontational. Make the children *want* to join in rather than tell them they ought to.

Purchasing or making your own instruments; what to collect

You will need a range of instruments which make a sound when shaken, when beaten or when scratched. Avoid blowing instruments which will need disinfecting each time they are used, unless the children bring their own. Your percussion instruments can be either untuned or tuned (xylophones or chime bars); I prefer the former since the sound matches any other sound and you do not hear clashes of harmony. Make sure you have enough instruments for all the children and adults in the group. If you have a particularly popular instrument (usually the biggest drum) try to save up for more than one or help the children take turns fairly. I usually break band time at least once to suggest to the children that they might like to choose a new instrument 'but only if you want to'.

Here is a possible shopping list if you are buying a set of percussion instruments. How many you buy will depend on the size of the group, but try to get a good range. You can opt for colourful plastic instruments (e.g. from the Early Learning Centre), or you can buy 'real' instruments which can have a better sound though are not so easily sucked, dropped or banged.

- Drums to beat with sticks e.g. snare drums
- Drums to beat with hands e.g. bongos
- Tambourines
- Jingle bells in rings and jingle bells on sticks
- Triangles; attach the beaters permanently with string
- Castanets
- Cabassa
- Guiro
- Wood blocks and beaters
- Indian bells
- Cymbals (to be used with careful supervision in order to protect noses and eyes)
- Maracas

If you decide to make your instruments, make sure beans and pulses are securely contained. Remember that some uncooked beans are poisonous and be wary of younger children swallowing loose small parts or ingredients. You can make a range of sounds with dry pasta, rice, beans, sand, broken shell and gravel. You can make drums with saucepan lids or metal bowls with wooden spoons, and make use of large used coffee tins which you can cover with bright paper or plastic. You will find further ideas in the resources listed at the back.

Chapter 4
Enjoying music together

In this chapter, you will find eight activities to help children 'warm up' to music time, to greet the children individually, and to say 'goodbye' at the end of the session. They are designed to build children's confidence and to form part of a regular routine in which children with learning difficulties can anticipate what is happening next.

Activity 4.1: Warming Up

Skill: To warm up and to join in at the beginning of a music session
Target link: G1 G2 G3 G4 L1 L2 V1 V5 M1 M2 S1 S2 S3 A3 A5 A7
Early Learning Goal link: PS1 PS4 LL1 LL6 LL13 PD1 CD4 CD8

What to do:
Arrange your space for music session (see Chapter 3). Call the children to sit down in a circle, and start playing an accompaniment or background music as you help them settle, in order to signal that it is music time and to hold their attention. As soon as they are gathered, sing a warm-up song. Always start with the same old favourite, though you might change this from term to term. This becomes an important cue for the child with learning difficulties that the familiar routine of music session is about to begin.

Choose a song with much repetition and simple actions e.g. 'If you're happy and you know it' (traditional; you will find the tune in *Apusskidu*).

If you're happy and you know it, clap your hands (x 2)
If you're happy and you know it, then you really want to show it
If you're happy and you know it, clap your hands.

Repeat with the simple actions 'wave your arms', 'stamp your feet', 'shout I AM'.

If a child has difficulties doing the actions, demonstrate them clearly, and ask the carer to place their hands gently over the child's to prompt. Alternatively, the carer can clap onto the child's hands, or wave at the child. Don't expect all children to manage the 'I AM' but be delighted if you get any vocalisation at all at this point.

Follow-up ideas:
- Look in *Okki-tokki-unga* for other very familiar and simple action rhymes.
- 'The wheels on the bus' is another firm favourite.
- Sometimes a child with special needs might use the action for, say, 'wheels on the bus' as a signal that he or she is looking forward to music.

The Music Makers Approach

Activity 4.2: Greeting Song

Skill: To encourage the children to greet each other at the start of the group
Target link: V1 V3 V5 V6 S6 U1 A1 A4 (waving 'hello')
Early Learning Goal link: PS1 PS2 PS3 PS4 PS13 LL1 LL6 CD4

What to do:

After the warm-up song, move straight into a greeting song. The aim is to greet each child by name, and encourage a look, a smile, a wave, or even a joining-in from the very confident ones. Let the children choose how they are going to respond, and do not expect them to sing or speak to you unless they feel ready to. This song is best sung unaccompanied so that you can move around the circle. Tell all the adults in the circle that they must sing too to keep you company! Move around the circle so that you can look each child in the face at their level. If a child has poor visual attention, give a touch on the shoulder or leg to engage attention.

This song can be sung to the tune of 'Peter Pointer, Peter Pointer, where are you?'

Jamie Briggs, Jamie Briggs, Where are you?
Here I am, Here I am, How do you do?

Put the child's own name into the first line. If you prefer to stick to first names, sing 'Hello Jamie, Hello Jamie' instead. If you have a very shy child who hides into a carer, sing 'There (s)he is, there (s)he is' so that (s)he is still included. As the children get more familiar with this greeting, encourage them all to wave at the child being greeted. This will help them learn each other's names.

Follow-up ideas:
- Use the children's names regularly before you talk to them in order to give respect and gain attention.
- Make sure you pronounce children's names correctly each time.
- Include any visiting babies and toddlers in your greeting song.
- If they enjoy it, sing the greeting song for certain children (for example, some children with language or communication difficulties) as they come in.

4. Enjoying music together

Activity 4.3: Old Macdonald's Makaton Farm

Skill: To help the children warm up using Makaton signs
Target link: G1 G2 G3 G4 L1 L2 V1 V5 M1 M2 S1 S2 S3 S4 A3 A5 A7
Early Learning Goal link: PS1 PS4 LL1 LL6 LL13 PD1 CD4 CD8

What to do:

Adopt this as one of your warm-ups if you have a child who is learning to use Makaton sign language, perhaps because of their speech and language difficulty or their hearing impairment. Talk to parents or visiting speech and language therapist about the signs the child is using, and ask them to demonstrate the signs used in this song. You might like to enquire from the therapist about possible Makaton courses in your area. Alternatively, introduce the signs as part of a topic on 'senses'. All the children will enjoy using action songs with the signs.

Sing 'Old Macdonald had a farm' (traditional). Stop at the point where you need to think of an animal, and invite suggestions. 'What does a *cow* say?' 'Can you remember the sign for *cow*?' Each verse, have just one animal and do not tax memories by building the animals up cumulatively at this stage.

- Makaton signs for cow: two fists on your brow, moving up in the shape of two horns
- Sheep: two fingers at the sides of your face moving outwards to draw a curly fleece
- Pig: a fist on your nose with a screwing movement
- Horse: two fingers astride one finger and trotting along
- Goat: pull your beard down
- Cat: preen your whiskers
- Dog: sit up and beg with two paws up
  (Ask parents for an actual demonstration)

Follow-up ideas:
- Ask the speech and language therapist about any Makaton videos.
- Use signing as a regular part of your playing and communication for those children who need it. Makaton is not used to replace spoken language but to encourage it and to make the child's communication clearer.
- Show the other children how to use the signs too.

The Music Makers Approach

Activity 4.4: The Shaking Game

Skill: To tune in to looking and listening at the beginning of a session, and to loosen up
Target link: L1 V2 V6 M2 M3 M4 M5 U9 A1 A2
Early Learning Goal link: PS4 PS5 PS15 LL1 PD1 PD2

What to do:

This is an excellent activity for encouraging the whole group to concentrate as one. You need a large tambourine. Tell the children that you are going to play some shaking music. When they hear it, they are to shake all over; shake their arms, shake their toes, shake their bodies all over. When it stops, they should stop too. Are they listening? Are they looking? Move round the circle as you shake the tambourine loudly, encouraging them to shake. Then beat the tambourine once loudly, stopping absolutely still. Praise children by name for looking and listening. Repeat three or four times, encouraging laughter and giggles as you shake, and scanning all the children's faces when you have stopped. Keep this fun and challenging. Pretend to put it away, but then let it shake just one last time. Praise all the children for looking and listening so well.

Follow-up ideas:
- Use other percussion instruments to suggest different actions e.g. a 'rainmaker' (broken shells and sand in a cylinder). When the children hear the rain, can they put their umbrellas up? When the rain stops, can they put them down again?
- Use this activity to introduce shaking percussion instruments at band time (see Chapter 9).

4. Enjoying music together

Activity 4.5: Jelly on a Plate

Skill: To lose inhibitions at the start of a session
Target link: L1 V2 V6 M2 M3 M4 M5 A1 A2
Early Learning Goal link: PS4 PS5 PS15 LL1 LL6 M5 PD1 PD2

What to do:

After a greeting song, move straight on to this chant. Encourage children to wobble all over when they say 'jelly' and 'wibble wobble'. Make this activity fun and do not be afraid to have a really good laugh together.

Jelly on a plate
Jelly on a plate
Wibble wobble, wibble wobble,
Jelly on a plate!

Move on straight away to another wobbling song: this one can be sung to the tune of 'Three blind mice'.

Three green jellyfish, three green jellyfish
Sat upon a rock, sat upon a rock
The first one felt like a swim, you know,
And slithered away to the sea, you know,
And left the rest on their own-i-o,
Just two green jellyfish.

Wobble all over for the 'jellyfish'. Raise your hands in the air and wobble them down all the way to the sea for the 'slithering'. Repeat one more time until there is one jellyfish left on the rock. Older children might like to act this out as you sing.

Follow-up ideas:
- Follow up later in the session by making jelly!
- For children who find it hard to move independently, give a gentle shake or tickle.

The Music Makers Approach

Activity 4.6: Everybody Clap Hands

Skill: To join in with a simple action at the beginning of the session
Target link: G1 G2 G3 G4 L1 L2 V2 V5 M1 M2 M3 A1 A3 A5
Early Learning Goal link: PS4 LL1 PD1 PD2 CD8

What to do:
Most very young children have great difficulty in both singing or attending to a rhyme and doing the actions at the same time. This is a good warm-up for getting *everyone* going in a simple and unchallenging clapping game. Choose a lively tape that they will all know, perhaps from a familiar jingle or video and all clap together, sharing your enjoyment of the tune. Keep this brief; about two verses at the most. Now that you have everyone's attention, carry on with the greeting song or the next action rhyme.

Follow-up ideas:
- Follow with a clapping action rhyme e.g.
  Pat-a-cake, pat-a-cake, baker's man,
  Bake me a cake as fast as you can,
  Prick it and pat it and mark it with 'B',
  Put it in the oven for baby and me.
        (traditional)

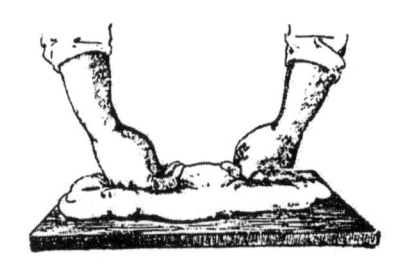

- Use clapping and cheering at the end of successful activities.
- Clap birthday ages together after singing 'Happy Birthday to you'.

4. Enjoying music together

Activity 4.7: It's Time to Say 'Goodbye'

Skill: To give a look, a smile or a wave when told 'goodbye'
Target link: V1 V3 V6 S6 U1 A1 A4
Early Learning Goal link: PS2 PS3 PS13 LL1 LL6 LL13

What to do:

Use this song to close your session. Sing the 'Goodbye song' below, moving round the circle as you sing. Encourage all the other adults and any children who can to join in the song too. As you reach each child, look them in the face, smile and sing the song, inserting their name. Encourage a look, a smile or a wave from each child. Some of the older or more confident children may well join in the 'goodbye'. If a child is very shy and hides their head, give a light touch to show that you respect and value them as you sing 'goodbye'.

In case you do not read music, the note names are written down so that you can pick the tune out on a keyboard, piano or recorder. Leave gaps for the dashes. An apostrophe after the note name (D') means top D. Work the tune out first so that you can use it confidently during the session.

```
It's time to say  Good-bye, it's time to say  Good-bye
D |B   B   A   A  |G - -  D |B   B   A   A  |G -
Good-bye,       Good-bye,      It's time to say  Good-bye.
D'|B  -   -   D'| B  -  -   D |B   B   A   A  |G
```

Follow-up ideas:
- There are some children with communication difficulties who learn to sing 'goodbye' before they can speak it. You might wish to sing 'goodbye' at other appropriate times too.
- Always get down to the child's level and greet or say 'goodbye' to the child with your full attention and respect.

Activity 4.8: Alternative Goodbye song

Skill: To give a look, a smile or a wave when told 'goodbye'
Target link: V1 V3 V6 S6 U1 A1 A4
Early Learning Goal link: PS2 PS3 PS13 LL1 LL6 LL13

What to do:

At the end of the session, sing this song to each child as you encourage a look, a wave or a smile (see activity 4.7). You can dismiss each child from the circle as you all sing 'goodbye' to them. Have another helper or two on hand to encourage the children who are leaving the circle to move to the next activity, drinks time etc.

The tune is the first two lines of 'Twinkle twinkle little star'. Substitute the child's name in the second line.

Now it's time to say Good-bye,
Sammy Dalton, off you fly!

Touch each child lightly to dismiss them, or shake hands as another variation (you need some sort of physical prompt to let them know when they can 'fly', or they will be up and off before they have looked at you and made their goodbyes).

Follow-up ideas:
- Some children might like to come with you on your journey around the circle, and do the shaking hands or waving with you. Limit this to one at a time.
- Look up other goodbye songs, or make these up, as substitutes. Do not change too often, in order to maintain familiarity.
- Another choice would be to sing this repeated phrase to each child, to the tune of 'Girls and boys come out to play' (traditional): 'Now is the end of music time, if you want to go and play that's fine!'

Chapter 5
Songs and action rhymes

In this chapter, you are encouraged to make use of the wealth of activity songs and rhymes generally available. You will find the resource list on page 76 helpful. There are eight suggestions to start you going, but please choose your action rhymes and songs flexibly and be looking out for new favourites all the time. Keep them simple, and do not expect all the children to manage complicated series of actions. Help children with physical difficulties make approximations of the action, gradually shaping up to closer matches.

Activity 5.1 The Monster Stomp

Skill: To join in a simple series of actions, including a one-two stepping rhythm
Target link: G2 G4 V5 V6 M1 M2 M3 M4 M5 M6 S1 A2 A7
Early Learning Goal link: PS1 PS4 PS14 LL8 LL13 PD1 PD2 PD3 CD9

What to do:
Look up 'The Monster Stomp' (*Stamp Your Feet Action Rhymes* by Sarah Hayes and Toni Goffe, Walker Books).

Chant it through first so that the children become familiar with the words and the rap rhythm. Make sure your adults know the words too. Use a one-two stepping and swaying movement for most of it, and 'wave your arms' and 'stamp your feet' at the appropriate time. 'Stretch them up' and 'put them to the ground' and encourage all the children to join in loudly for the 'ooh-ah' monster sounds. Children really enjoy this one. Finish by coming into the circle together with a roar.

Make allowances for what movements any children with physical disabilities can make, so that you can find some kind of monster moves they can do too. For children at an earlier stage of development, move their legs or arms in a one-two rhythm, and bounce them on a knee. Be aware of any timid children who might need additional reassurance.

Follow-up ideas:
- Look for other action rhymes with a one-two rhythm, such as 'One, two, buckle my shoe' (traditional).

Activity 5.2: Everybody Copy Me

Skill: To imitate a simple action
Target link: G2 G3 G4 L6 V1 V5 V6 M3 M4 A1 A3 A4 A7
Early Learning Goal link: PS1 PS4 PS8 LL1 LL6 LL13 PD2 CD3

What to do:

The tune is the same as for 'Everybody do this' (by Mary Miller) which you will find in *Okki-tokki-unga*. Tell the children you are going to sing a copying song. Choose a very simple action to start with, like clapping hands, holding arms up, touching noses, swinging legs. Sing the song and model the action for children to copy.

Everybody copy, copy, copy,
Everybody copy, copy ... (child's name).

You will find the older children singing as well as doing the actions, but the younger children will just copy what you are doing. Some children who might find this difficult will need a grown-up to encourage them to look and to prompt an approximate version of the action, hand-over-hand if need be.

After two or three goes, invite any child who wants to choose an action for you all to copy. This activity is excellent for boosting self-esteem. Make sure you include children with restricted movements or ideas so that you can give value to their choices and abilities.

Follow-up ideas:
- Play 'follow-my-leader' later on in the session.
- Spend individual time with a child who has difficulties in copying, teaching them how to imitate. Keep your movements large and exaggerated so that it is very clear what the child needs to copy. Use mirror play to reinforce this. Prompt the child to do the actions if you need to, praising warmly for co-operation or success.

5. Songs and action rhymes

Activity 5.3: Benjie Hammers with One Hammer

Skill: To imitate a simple action number rhyme
Target link: G2 G3 L1 V1 V3 V5 V6 M1 M3 S8 U1 A1 A7
Early Learning Goal link: PS4 LL1 LL6 M2 M5 M11 PD1 CD8

What to do:

You will find a version of this rhyme in *Okki-tokki-unga*. I like the version where 'Benjie goes to sleep now' and then 'Benjie's waking up now' at the end.

Benjie hammers with one hammer, one hammer, one hammer
Benjie hammers with one hammer, all day long.
Benjie hammers with two hammers ... (etc., up to five hammers).

Children with physical difficulties will need help and prompting to beat with one or two hammers. Instead of expecting them to hammer with fists, feet and head all at once (for five hammers), just concentrate on the part of the body not yet used so that you practise these movements:

Verse 1: hammer with one fist
Verse 2: hammer with the other fist
Verse 3: swing or hammer with one leg
Verse 4: swing or hammer with the other leg
Verse 5: shake or nod the head

Your older or more physically able children will be able to join all the movements together as the verses build up. Thus, once again, you have an activity which includes all your children but at different levels of ability and joining-in.

As you all go to sleep, encourage the children to 'lie *down*' (or to put heads down and snuggle in if they are on a parent's knee). Leave a moment or two of silence to encourage quietness, listening and anticipation. Then sing the last waking-up verse briskly as you all 'hammer all over again!'

Follow-up idea:
- Sing 'Nick-nack-paddywack, give your dog a bone' (traditional).

The Music Makers Approach

Activity 5.4: Row, Row, Row Your Boat

Skill: To work with a partner, imitating a rocking action
Target link: G3 L6 V3 M1 M3 A1 A2
Early Learning Goal link: PS2 PS4 PS12 LL13 PD2

What to do:

You will be familiar with this traditional rhyme; if you need to, ask a colleague for the tune.

Row, row, row your boat, gently down the stream,
Merrily, merrily, merrily, merrily, life is but a dream.

The first time you sing this, allow the children to rock in their places as if they are rowing a boat. Children on knees can be rocked gently.

When the children are more familiar with the song, encourage them to join in pairs, facing each other and rocking gently forwards and backwards as they hold hands. Children with particular needs can be helped by a grown-up sitting behind them, legs either side on the floor. Alternatively, younger children can be sat astride a knee with a grown-up as partner. Always aim for helping children join in fully with another child if at all possible.

Another variation for this song has as its last verses:

Row, row, row your boat, gently down the stream,
If you see a crocodile, don't forget to scream!
                (Everybody screams!)

Row, row, row your boat, gently down the stream,
If you see a tall giraffe, don't forget to laugh!
                (Everybody laughs!)

Follow-up ideas:
- Try back-to-back rocking.
- Place all the children in a long line, sitting on the floor with legs each side of the child in front. Now row your long boat together!

5. Songs and action rhymes

Activity 5.5: Incy Wincy Spider

Skill: To look and copy a simple series of actions
Target link: V5 V6 S6 A1 A2 A6 A7
Early Learning Goal link: LL1 LL6 LL13 KW1 PD2

What to do:
This is just one example of how you can use rhymes and chants to encourage actions. Again, try to choose activities which allow everyone to join in within their own capabilities. In this rhyme, for example, some children will be able to copy a quite complicated finger to thumb 'climbing' movement as Incy climbs up the spout. Other children will, more simply, raise their arms in the air.

> Incy Wincy Spider climbed up the water spout,
> Down came the rain and washed poor Incy out.
> Out came the sunshine and dried up all the rain,
> So Incy Wincy Spider climbed up the spout again.
> (traditional)

Make your fingers climb upwards in the first line. Then let them fall with a sprinkling movement for the rain, washing Incy away. Let your hands lift again to trace the shape of the sun and move upwards as the rain dries. Then climb your fingers upwards again for the final line. For children at a much earlier stage in their development, their grown-up can use their own fingers to climb up the child.

Follow-up ideas:
- Make dangly spiders to jiggle during this song.
- Link to the rainmaker game (4.4).

Activity 5.6: The Grand Old Duke of York

Skill: To learn the actions for 'up' and 'down'
Target link: G3 G4 V5 V6 M3 U4 A7
Early Learning Goal link: PS4 LL1 LL13 M1 KW7 PD2 CD4 CD8

What to do:

See whether you can find someone to accompany you on an instrument to make this song go with a strong rhythm; otherwise, have a grown-up beat a drum or a tambourine as you sing. Encourage the children to raise their arms *up* in the air as the Duke of York marches *up* the hill, and *down* to the ground as he marches *down* again.

Oh, the Grand Old Duke of York,
He had ten thousand men,
He marched them up to the top of the hill,
And he marched them down again,
And when they were up, they were up,
And when they were down, they were down,
And when they were only half way up,
They were neither up nor down.

(traditional)

Follow-up ideas:
- Encourage the children to join in a long line raising arms *up* and *down* as you lead them, still singing the song. Look for ways of including non-ambulant children too.
- Use a variation of this at band time, bending low and reaching high as you march with the instruments (see Chapter 9).
- Alternatively, play your instruments loudly as you climb 'up' the hill and softly as you come 'down'.

5. Songs and action rhymes

Activity 5.7: Jack-in-the-Box

Skill: To listen out for a key word and then respond
Target link: G3 G4 V5 V6 M3 S6 U4 A7
Early Learning Goal link: PS4 LL1 LL13 M1 KW7 PD2 CD4 CD8

What to do:

Encourage all the children to make themselves as small as possible, with their heads down low. When the song reaches the word '*up*', encourage everyone to sit up tall and follow the actions in the song. Push children's heads down gently on the second last line, or encourage them to push their own or a neighbour's. Wag your finger at the children on the last line. If you stay in a sitting position throughout this song, non-ambulant children can join in the same way as the others.

The words fit approximately to the tune 'Girls and boys come out to play'.

Jack-in-the-box jumps up in the air,
He waves his arms and he waggles his hair,
Then I push him down again,
Saying 'Jack-in-the-box, go back-in-your-box!'

Follow-up idea:
- Show the children a real Jack-in-the-box (beware the rather startling cry that some models make).

The Music Makers Approach

Activity 5.8: The Wheels on the Bus

Skill: To join in a familiar action song
Target link: G1 G3 G4 V1 V5 V6 M2 M3 M4 S2 S3 S5 A1 A3 A4 A7
Early Learning Goal link: PS4 LL6 LL13 KW1 PD2

What to do:

You are sure to be familiar with this song, and it makes a very good warm up song too. The main thing is to choose actions which everyone can do, whatever their ability. You may be able to target particular actions that some of the children with special needs are currently mastering, such as clapping hands or waving bye-bye.

Here are some ideas for keeping the actions simple:

The children on the bus go wriggle, wriggle, wriggle ...
The mums on the bus go tickle, tickle, tickle ...
The people on the bus all wave goodbye ...
The babies on the bus all clap their hands ...

Sometimes, children with speech and language difficulties might be practising certain sounds with their speech and language therapist. These exercises might be built in to a song like this, for example:

The birds in the trees go la la la ...
The babies on the bus go wa wa wa ...
The engine on the bus goes pu pu pu ...
The doors on the bus go hisssss ...

I usually accelerate the last verse as the driver goes 'brm brm brm' and as we steer our steering wheels round the corners.

Follow-up ideas:
- Encourage the children to think of their own verses.
- Sing 'The children in playgroup go ...' (etc.).
- Arrange chairs in the centre for some of the children to sit on the bus.

Chapter 6
Looking and listening games

In this chapter, there are eight activities which encourage the children to look, to listen and to attend in a group situation. Music tends to be particularly motivating and enjoyable, and so it makes it easier for children to attend, to join in and to behave appropriately in the group.

Activity 6.1: Find the Sound

Skill: To turn towards a sound
Target link: L1 L5 V2 V4 U9
Early Learning Goal link: PS5 LL1 PD3 CD1

What to do:
Choose another grown-up to help you. One of you pick up a tambourine and shake it so that the children can see it and hear it. Tell them what it is called, and pass it round the circle for everyone to have a go. The other should pick up the jingle bells and do likewise. Now stand outside the circle, one of you at each end.

Tell the children that you are going to hide your instruments behind your backs and take it in turns to shake it. Can the children guess where the sound is coming from?

Wink at your colleague so that (s)he plays the instrument, shaking it behind a back. Invite the children to 'find the sound'. Wait until almost all eyes are turned to the correct place, then reveal the instrument and shake it again so that they can all see. Praise their looking and their listening. Have about two goes each, varying which of you plays.

Follow-up ideas:
- Select different pairs of instruments.
- Invite a further helper and instrument to make the task more challenging. Build up to three or four sounds.

The Music Makers Approach

Activity 6.2: The Pointing Game

Skill: To point towards a sound
Target link: L1 L5 V2 V4 U9 I1 I2
Early Learning Goal link: PS5 LL1 PD3 CD1

What to do:

In this game, you take it in turns to be in the middle of the circle. It is best if you have the first go so that the children can understand what to do. Tie a loose scarf around your head, or hold a pad to your face so that you cannot see. Make sure another grown-up in the circle helps the children. They should choose an instrument, and pass it from person to person around the circle, each one making a sound with it. The person in the centre must try to point to where the sound is coming from as it passes around the circle.

Follow-up ideas:
- If a child is worried about covering their eyes, try offering them a woolly hat to pull down, or a soft toy to burrow into.
- Use a signal to make the instrument change directions from time to time.
- Have two instruments at different points of the circle. Invite the child in the middle to say, 'point to the drum' or 'point to the bells'.

6. Looking and listening games

Activity 6.3: Feely Bag

Skill: To use touch and sound to identify a musical instrument
Target link: L1 L5 V2 V4 U9 I1 I2
Early Learning Goal link: PS5 LL1 PD3 CD1 CD5

What to do:

Show the children three instruments, perhaps a tambourine, the bells and the castanets. Pass them each round the circle and let the children make a sound with them. Now tell the children that you are going to hide them all inside a bag. Choose a big draw-string bag that you can easily reach inside. Place all three instruments inside. Now reach in and play one of them. 'Would anyone like to come and feel inside the bag for the right instrument?' Alternatively, invite a child to pull the instruments out one at a time and play them one after the other, asking 'Was it that one?'

For children who have difficulties in remembering, have two of each instrument and continue to play one whilst they feel inside the bag for its like.

Follow-up ideas:
- Play 'sound lotto' games.
- Make your own tape of familiar musical instruments and invite the children to identify or match them to encourage links between listening and looking.

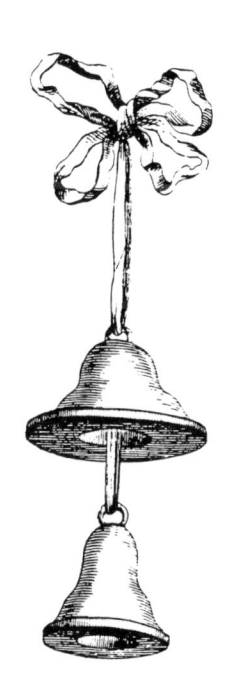

The Music Makers Approach

Activity 6.4: A Listening Walk

Skill: To listen to sounds and identify them in the environment
Target link: L1 L5 V2 V4 U9
Early Learning Goal link: PS5 LL1 LL5 PD3 CD1 CD10

What to do:
  Tell the children you are all going on a listening walk. This can be indoors or outside; if indoors, you will need to think ahead of certain sounds the children will be able to identify (the cars outside, the drip of a tap, the bubbles of the fish tank, the singing of children in the hall, the tune of a radio, the clatter of the bricks...). Lead them off and choose different places to stop. Invite the children to shut their eyes and talk together about all that you can hear.

Follow-up ideas:
- Make your own tape recording of familiar household sounds (a lavatory flushing, a kettle boiling, a hoover, a washing machine, a telephone ringing, a doorbell...) and see if the children can identify them. You could also match these to pictures or to real items. See page 76 for further resource suggestions.
- Use the instruments to provide sound effects for a short story.

6. Looking and listening games

Activity 6.5: The Dinosaur Hunt

Skill: To listen to, and repeat short phrases and to remember a sequence of actions
Target link: G2 G4 V6 A2 A3 A7
Early Learning Goal link: PS4 PS7 PS19 LL5 PD1 PD2

What to do:

Wait until the children are really confident; most of them love this activity. Hide a plastic dinosaur somewhere in the room so that you can 'find it' at the end of the dinosaur hunt. Make sure that all the children have a chance to join in, regardless of mobility. Tell the children what you are going to do. Everything you say, they are to repeat. Make sure you have plenty of grown-ups to help the children copy you.

'We're going on a dinosaur hunt' (they repeat as you all march round)
'I'm not scared' (they repeat as you all point to yourselves proudly)
'Beautiful day' (they repeat as you all point up to the clear sky)
'Oh oh...' (they repeat as you all stop still)
'Grass' (they repeat)
'Tall, wavy grass' (they repeat as you all make a swishing hand movement)
'You can't go over it' (they repeat as you all make a gesture or sound for 'over')
'You can't go under it' (they repeat as you all gesture 'under')
'Got to go through it' (they repeat) (All make huge steps, saying 'swish swish swish')

Verse 2: 'mud, dark squelchy mud' : make squelchy wellington-boot steps
Verse 3: 'nettles, tall stingy nettles': jump over them going 'ow! ow! ow!'
Verse 4: 'a cave, a dark echoey cave': feel your way in making echo noises.
Verse 5: 'a dinosaur! Let's run home!': reverse all the sounds as you run back to base. First make echoey noises, then nettles, then mud, tall wavy grass, and then arrive safely home and celebrate.

Follow-up idea:
- Invite the children to help you make up new verses.

The Music Makers Approach

Activity 6.6: Hunt the Mouse

Skill: To discriminate between loud and soft sound
Target link: L1 L7 V5 U6
Early Learning Goal link: PS5 LL1 CD1 CD4

What to do:

This is a variation of the traditional party game 'Hunt the thimble'. Invite one child to have the first go. Have one grown-up lead the child away just whilst you hide the toy mouse (or whatever you decide to hunt). Sit the children in a circle and give the toy to one child to hide within their clothing. Make sure all the children except the seeker have seen where it is hidden, focusing the attention of any children who have difficulty in noticing things.

Now invite your seeker back into the room. Tell him/her that one of the children is hiding the toy. Let the other grown-up lead him/her around the inside of the circle whilst the rest of you sing loudly 'How *warm* you are, how *warm* you are, how *warm* you are, how *warm*' (to the tune of 'Auld Lang's Syne') or indeed 'How *cold* you are...' sung softly, depending on whether the seeker is close to or far away from the toy. You should be able to make it very obvious from your exaggerated response when the seeker is standing in front of the correct child. Invite him/her to tap the shoulder and the child tapped should reveal whether or not they are hiding the toy. This can generate tremendous giggling!

Follow-up ideas:
- Play 'hunt the thimble' (or similar) around the room, using progressively smaller objects which have to be looked for carefully.
- Repeat the louds and softs with musical instruments instead of singing.

6. Looking and listening games

Activity 6.7: Swanee Whistles

Skill: To discriminate between high and low sounds
Target link: L1 V6 U4 U5 A6
Early Learning Goal link: LL1 CD1 CD4

What to do:

You will need a swanee whistle for this activity; one of those whistles that makes a sliding high-low note. It is possible to use other instruments (a glockenspiel, a keyboard, a mouth organ, and we used a trombone once!)

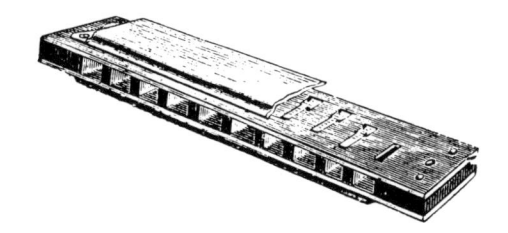

Invite the children to listen to the sound. When it goes *high*, they should raise their hands *up* in the air. When it goes *low*, they should hold their hands *down* low. Children find this very hard, and they will need your demonstration at first.

Start off slowly raising and lowering the note. When they get more confident, catch them out by some quick changes.

Invite some of your less confident children to make the whistle sound for the rest of the group to respond to; use a medi-wipe or a disinfectant wipe to keep mouth-pieces hygienic between children.

Follow-up ideas:
- Invite children to tell you if you are playing your tuned instrument *high* or *low*.
- Invite them to raise and lower arms as you play *high up* or *down low*.
- Play with making high squeaky voices and low growly voices. Use these as effects at story time.

The Music Makers Approach

Activity 6.8: Pass the Sound

Skill: To practise handling objects carefully and gently and to locate sounds
Target link: L1 L7 V2 V6 U6 I1 I10
Early Learning Goal link: PS4 PS13 PD3 PD4 CD1 CD4

What to do:

Choose a musical instrument which makes a sound as you pass it, perhaps a tambourine or some jingle bells. Find an extra helper to allow you to close your eyes and play a guessing game.

Tell the children you are going to play a game passing the instrument round the circle. First, invite them to pass it as noisily as possible. Then challenge them to pass it very gently and quietly without any sound at all. When the children are managing this, sit outside with your eyes closed and see if you can point to where you think the instrument has got to. Praise them constantly for being so quiet and gentle.

Place your helper next to the younger children to help and encourage them and allow your older children to take a turn guessing.

Follow-up ideas:
- Practise playing instruments *loudly* and *quietly*.
- Practise singing *loudly* and *quietly*.
- Follow up with these words in the rest of the session; challenge children to close a door *quietly* or walk past another classroom *quietly*.

Chapter 7
Movement and rhythm games

Here, you will find eight activities which encourage children to enjoy movement and to listen to rhythm and beat. Children with mobility and co-ordination difficulties often feel less inhibited and challenged when moving to a musical activity.

Activity 7.1: Drum Beats

Skill: To copy the rhythm of your name
Target link: G3 L6 V3 V6 U1 A1 I3 I6
Early Learning Goal link: LL13 LL14 PD6 CD4

What to do:

This activity makes a good greeting activity too. You will need a large drum; a large tambour or bodhran is excellent, but other drums can be used too.

Invite the children to beat their first names on the drum. Show them what you mean.

Say 'Hello Phil-ip', 'Hello Car-ol-ine', 'Hello Ah-hyun', beating the syllables of the names as you say them. Now move around the circle, giving the beater to each child, and saying 'Hello ...', encouraging them to beat their names to you.

The joy of this activity is that you should be able to guarantee total success, regardless of level of ability. Some children will manage this activity all by themselves, and even be able to tackle their full names with practice. Others will need you to whisk the drum away after the correct number of beats and therefore succeed with your help.

For children who find it hard to hold a beater, a hand or fist could be used instead, perhaps with a physical prompt (hand-over-hand) from the parent or helper.

Follow-up ideas:
- Always have a strong drum beat from one of the grown-ups at marching and band time.
- Have sufficient drums for everyone to feel they get a regular 'go' at band time; they tend to be the most popular instrument. Make sure the quieter and shyer children have a chance to make a lot of noise too.

Activity 7.2: Cobbler, Cobbler

Skill: To move to a simple one-two rhythm
Target link: G3 G4 L6 M1 M3 M4 M5 A1
Early Learning Goal link: LL1 LL13 LL14 PD1 CD4 CD5

What to do:
You will need a visual prop here; try to get hold of some big work boots or heavy shoes. Encourage all the children to kneel down in a circle with their two hands on the floor. Put your two hands in your heavy boots, and raise them up and down to tramp a strong one-two rhythm. Can the children make the same rhythm? (If you have the time, they could all take shoes off and put them on their hands, kneeling.) Chant this traditional rhyme as you 'walk' your hands.

> Cobbler, cobbler, mend my shoe,
> Get it done by half past two.
> (traditional)

or

> Down at the bottom of the deep blue sea,
> Catching fishes for my tea,
> How many fishes can you see?
> One...two...three...
> (traditional)

Children at a younger stage of physical development might enjoy having arms or legs swung to the beat, or bouncing when held in a standing position.

Follow-up ideas:
- Look for other rhymes or songs with a steady marching rhythm e.g. The Monster Stomp (activity 5.1), the Grand Old Duke of York (5.6), Nick-nack-paddywack (to a slow rhythm), etc.
- Choose some tunes with a strong one-two rhythm at marching time. Use a loud drum to keep the beat, or stamp with your booted feet as you lead the march.

7. Movement and rhythm games

Activity 7.3: Musical Bumps and Old Favourites

Skill: To start and stop moving to music
Target link: G2 L3 L4 V5 M2 M6 U5
Early Learning Goal link: PS1 LL1 PD1 PD2 CD9

What to do:
These activities are almost too obvious to include, but they are old favourites for the children and do encourage independent movement, looking and listening. Your task is to think of all your children, regardless of need, and plan how you can include them within their own abilities.

- Musical Bumps: play a musical tape, and encourage the children to flop to the floor when the music stops.
- Musical Statues: encourage the children to keep still when the music stops.
- Musical Partners: encourage the children to hold hands with a partner when the music stops (make sure there is an even number of children).
- Musical Hats: encourage the children to put on a hat when the music stops (have enough for everyone and spread them out over your floor area).
- Musical Instruments: encourage the children to choose a musical instrument when the music stops, and play the tape for a short passage whilst they play them.

These versions are not competitive, and no-one is 'out'. However, you should be able to involve all the children, and also find some good mixing together of all the children in the process.

Follow-up ideas:
- What other musical party games could be adapted to encourage movement, looking and listening? Pass the Teddy (instead of Parcel), The Farmer's in his Den, Ring-o-ring-o-roses (which can be played in a sitting position if some of the children are non-ambulant, dropping your arms to the floor for 'all fall down'). This can also lead into the one-two rhythm you have been practising in activity 7.2.

The Music Makers Approach

Activity 7.4: The Kangaroo Song

Skill: To bounce to the rhythm of a beat, and have fun in movement
Target link: G2 L6 V5 M1 M5
Early Learning Goal link: PS1 LL13 PD1 CD9

What to do:

This is a very enjoyable activity which children can join in with in a variety of ways. Older and physically able children can bounce to the beat. Other children can bounce in a standing position whilst being supported, or can be bounced on a knee.

Any bouncy music will do, though you will find the 'Kangaroo song' in *Apusskidu* (by Virginia Pavelko and L.B. Scott) particularly useful. The children should sit still for the verse, but can bounce in the air for the chorus. Repeat the song two or three times. If you feel that the children are getting very excited, try this with a smaller group, or see if they can sit on the floor and pretend their hands are the kangaroos.

Follow-up ideas:
- Look for pieces of music with a bouncy, light beat to move to.
- Look up songs about 'Noah's Ark' or zoos to follow the animal theme, e.g., 'The animals went in two by two' (traditional) or 'Daddy's taking us to the zoo tomorrow' (Tom Paxton), both in *Apusskidu*.

7. Movement and rhythm games

Activity 7.5: Five Little Speckled Frogs

Skill: To make a movement to a key word
Target link: G3 M1 M5 S8 U8 A2
Early Learning Goal link: LL1 LL13 M2 M8 KW1 PD2 CD4

What to do:

Look for 'Five Little Speckled Frogs' from *Apusskidu*. Ask children to volunteer to be one of the five frogs who should crouch in the middle of the circle. You will find that you need to crouch there too to lead the actions. For children with mobility problems, invite them to make their hands into the jumping frogs or give them bean bags to toss upwards at the key words.

When you reach the word '*jumped*', then all the frogs should jump from a crouching position into the air. Pause the song at the end of each verse to count on your fingers how many frogs are left. Encourage the children to hold out their fingers to count, with a grown-up sitting close to prompt children who need help.

Follow-up ideas:
- Look for songs that require actions to certain key words e.g. 'All fall *down*'. Encourage those children who have limited understanding to anticipate the actions, or to join in with the key word.
- Chant '*Five* fat sausages sizzling in the pan, all of a sudden one went *bang*!', clapping on the bang and, again, counting fingers between verses. When you get to '*No* fat sausages sizzling in the pan', chant this verse in a whisper and finish with 'But all of a sudden the pan went *BANG*!'
- For children with short attention spans, start at three and work downwards.

The Music Makers Approach

Activity 7.6 Heads, Shoulders, Knees and Toes

Skill: To point to different body points
Target link: G3 V5 V6 M3 U2 A1
Early Learning Goal link: PS4 LL1 KW5 PD1 PD2 CD4

What to do:

This activity is included to show how a very familiar rhyme or song can be adapted to include all children regardless of need.

You are likely to be familiar with this traditional tune:

Heads, shoulders, knees and toes, knees and toes,
Heads, shoulders, knees and toes, knees and toes,
Eyes and ears, and mouth and nose,
Heads, shoulders, knees and toes, knees and toes.
          (traditional)

Start very slowly indeed, and allow most of the children to join in independently from the start, copying your actions as you point to each body part on yourself.

Pair each child who is still learning body parts with a grown-up or parent. The first time through, the helper should point to each part mentioned on the child, emphasising the key word, 'Head ... shoulder ... knees ... toes ... eyes ... ears ... mouth ... nose ...'

The second time through, take it just as slow, but ask the helpers to encourage (hand-over-hand if necessary) the child to point to themselves.

The third time through, take it at a tremendous rate for fun. The helpers should do the pointing again onto their child, ending with a laugh and a tickle. Meanwhile the children who are joining in the activity independently, will have the challenge of doing so very quickly.

Follow-up ideas:
- Look in Chapter 8 for more activities which help the teaching of body parts.
- Build in body parts to the introduction song, 'If you're happy and you know it, touch your *head*' (etc.).

7. Movement and rhythm games

Activity 7.7: The Crocodile Song

Skill: To recognise body parts and to change positions
Target link: G2 V1 U2 A7 M2 M3 M4
Early Learning Goal link: PS1 LL1 LL13 KW6 PD1

What to do:

This favourite activity has been included for older children; not for the faint-hearted, this one!

Gather in a circle. Start by standing, though look for ways of including children who cannot stand too (they will need a parent or helper to help them get into different positions). Hold hands and swing arms as you sing the chorus. The tune is the same as 'In and out the dusty bluebells'.

I'm being eaten by a great big crocodile,
I'm being eaten by a great big crocodile,
I'm being eaten by a great big crocodile,
I don't like it at all!

Now say, 'Oh no! He's eaten my toe!' and get onto your knees.

Repeat the chorus from your new position, inserting these verses after each chorus:

'Oh my! He's got my thigh!' (lie on tummies but push up from the waist)
'Oh lummy! He's got my tummy!' (lie prone with head pushed up)
'I think I'm dead! He's got my head!' (lie flat on your tummies)
'Hurray we shout! He's spat me out!' (up you all get)

(With acknowledgements to the Folk Camp Society where I first heard this.)

Follow-up ideas:
- Look for ways of adapting other traditional circle dances to include all the children e.g. 'Here we go looby loo', 'Hokey Cokey', 'In and out the dusty bluebells', 'Wind the bobbin up', 'One two three four five six seven'.

The Music Makers Approach

Activity 7.8: Dinner on the Train

Skill: To move faster and slower to a spoken rhythm
Target link: G2 G4 V5 V6 M1 M2 M3 M4 M5 M6 M7 S1 A1
Early Learning Goal link: PS4 LL8 LL13 LL14 PD1 PD2 CD1 CD4

What to do:

This is a good activity to insert just before marching time when you are already in a long line. Think ahead about how you are going to involve children with a range of needs. Children who are standing with support but not yet walking may like to bounce in a standing position and supported by a grown-up in the centre of the ring.

Tell the children that you are going on a pretend train journey. You are going to have your dinner on the train, but it's a very funny dinner because it's back to front! Can they copy what you do?

Chant these words to sound like a steam train gathering momentum. Churn your arms like the pistons on the wheels, and move faster as it goes.

Cof-fee, cof-fee,
cof-fee, cof-fee,
Cheese and biscuits, cheese and biscuits,
cheese and biscuits, cheese and biscuits,
Chocolate pudding, chocolate pudding,
chocolate pudding, chocolate pudding,
Bangers and mash, bangers and mash,
bangers and mash, bangers and mash,
SOOOOOOOOOOOOOUP!

Follow-up ideas:
- Sing other train songs e.g. 'The wheels on the train go round and round'.
- If one of the children is learning how to blow, invite them to blow a whistle to start the train.
- Make a chant together out of other words which have distinct rhythms.

Chapter 8
Concepts and understanding

This chapter contains eight activities which encourage children's understanding of keywords and concepts. Children with learning and language difficulties may find it particularly hard to understand abstract concepts and these activities aim to link concept with action in a concrete way.

Activity 8.1: Favourite Colours

Skill: To look for and identify a named colour
Target link: V5 V6 U7
Early Learning Goal link: PS8 KW7 KW12 CD2

What to do:
Tell the children you are going to sing a song together all about colours. This song fits to the first four lines of the 'Eton Boating Song':

I have a favourite colour,
My favourite colour is *red*,
Red is the colour that *Jonathan* wears,
Everyone look for *red*.

When you reach the words in italics, add the name of one of the children who is wearing a lot of a particular colour. Stop the song while you help all the children look for the colour red on their clothing. Show them the colour on your own clothing that matches. Point out children who are wearing similar clothes. Ask whose favourite colour red is. Repeat the song for a new colour and a new child. Encourage the children to join in once they know the song. Encourage them to help each other find the colours and make sure each child feels included.

Help the younger children to look for the colours. They may find it easier to find a piece of clothing which *matches* a colour you show them, rather than to pick a colour out from its name alone.

Follow-up ideas:
- Introduce songs about rainbows.
- Comment on the colours in the children's clothes as you greet them; 'Hello, Peter, you *are* wearing a lot of red today. I think we ought to sing the colour song!'

The Music Makers Approach

Activity 8.2: Four Currant Buns

Skill: To join in a simple number rhyme
Target link: S1 S6 S8 U8
Early Learning Goal link: M6 M8 LL13

What to do:
You may know this traditional rhyme which you can chant together.

Four currant buns in a baker's shop,
Round and fat with sugar on the top,
Along came ... (child's name) with a penny one day,
Bought a currant bun and took it away.
                              (traditional)

You can substitute a different child's name for each verse. Pause between each verse to hold up and count fingers (or for a grown-up to touch and count fingers on a child who needs help), and repeat the verse until there are no buns left. You can also play this with real props of buns or card pictures.

Follow-up ideas:
- There is a wealth of counting rhymes available. Keep them simple, e.g. only going up to three at first, and gradually building up to five. If you are starting at five, invite the children to 'show me five' first by holding up a hand with fingers splayed.
- Play a partner hand game; 'Give me five, on the side, in the air, down below' etc.
- For children at a very early stage, start with:

Two little dickey birds sitting on the wall,
One called Peter, the other called Paul,
Fly away Peter, fly away Paul,
Come back Peter, come back Paul.
                              (traditional)

8. Concepts and understanding

Activity 8.3: Nose, Nose, Show Me Your Nose

Skill: To point to named body parts
Target link: V5 V6 U2 A1 A7
Early Learning Goal link: LL1 LL6 LL13

What to do:

You can easily make up your own verses which emphasise key words for children who might have difficulties in understanding them, or in selecting them out from long strings of words. These words were made up by parents and professionals in our child development centre group because we found that most action songs made the key words easy to miss. The tune is written out in a similar form to that used in activity 4.7.

Nose, nose, show me your *nose,*
G - - |C - - |G E C | D -
The colder it is the more it blows!
D | C C C | D E F | E - D | C - -

Before each verse stop to invite all the children to point to the body part mentioned, prompting any children who need it. Repeat with other verses such as:

Ear, ear, show me an *ear,*
They hold on my specs and they help me to hear!
and
Tummy, tummy, show me your *tummy,*
I'll give it a tickle and make it feel funny! (etc.)

Follow-up ideas:
- Look for other songs and action rhymes with body parts in them.
- Use the 'Everybody copy' rhyme (activity 5.2) to copy pointing to different body parts.
- Play a game seeing what sounds the children can make with their hands and their feet.

The Music Makers Approach

Activity 8.4: Goldilocks

Skill: To listen and respond to a simple story-song
Target link: G3 V1 V6 A1 A7
Early Learning Goal link: LL1 LL5 LL6 LL13 M2

What to do:

This song provides a wealth of learning opportunities for different ages and stages. You will find the song in *Okki-tokki-unga*. Again, if you find singing difficult, you can speak this as a rhyme but you will have to work a little harder to hold their interest. Alternatively, start the activity by telling the children a simple version of this familiar fairy tale.

The children will be most interested if you arrange some props. For example, you can have three teddy bears in three different sizes, and three chairs, three bowls, three toy beds of equivalent sizes. Steady the song up at the end of each verse as you count 'One...two...three'.

To keep this song simple when working with children of mixed ability, I usually keep the same three actions for 'huge', 'small' and 'tiny', starting with my arms wide apart and ending with my hands close together. If you are telling the story instead of singing the song, use the same hand actions as you come to the appropriate parts of the story.

Encourage the children to match the props to the right bear as the story or song progresses, so that they have to think carefully about grading sizes.

Follow-up ideas:
- Have a music session based on bears (or other 'cuddlies') and invite each child to bring along their particular favourite that day. Select teddies to join in this song. Use the 'teds' to sing 'Miss Polly had a dolly' (traditional), to point to body parts, to rock for 'Rock-a-bye baby' or 'Row, row, row the boat' etc.

8. Concepts and understanding

Activity 8.5: This Is the Way

Skill: To think about sequences of actions
Target link: G3 V5 V6 A7
Early Learning Goal link: LL8 KW1 PD1

What to do:
Tell the children you are going to sing a song all about getting up in the morning. What do the children do when they wake? Prompt replies such as 'get out of bed', 'wash my face', 'brush my teeth', 'have my breakfast', 'put on my clothes', 'go to playgroup' etc.

Now build their answers into a 'getting up song', using the tune of 'Here we go round the mulberry bush'. Ask the children for ideas about how to mime each action, then sing the song together. Here is one example:

This is the way I get out of bed ...
This is the way I wash my face ...
This is the way I pull on my tee-shirt ...
This is the way I eat my toast ...
This is the way I brush my teeth ...etc.

Follow-up ideas:
- If you listen to children's song tapes and look through your resources, you will find other songs about sequences of actions.
- Sing a similar song about your pre-school, inviting ideas from the children about activities and mimed actions to build in to it, telling all about their day there.

The Music Makers Approach

Activity 8.6: Musical Positions

Skill: To understand and respond to preposition words; 'in front of', 'behind', 'in', 'on' and 'under'
Target link: G4 A1 U4
Early Learning Goal link: M2 PD3 CD2

What to do:

This is one way of making it more fun to put away your musical instruments after band time. Otherwise, you can do this activity separately. Perhaps keep it to five or six goes, choosing different children and prepositions each time, but always including any child with difficulties in understanding so that they can have extra practice.

Put a small but solid box with a lid in the centre of the circle. Invite a child to put their instrument 'in front of the box', 'behind the box', 'in the box', 'on the box', or 'under the box'. Keep this challenging and fun, and stay close to prompt the correct action. Invite the other children to cheer and clap as soon as the instrument is placed correctly.

For the child needing the extra practice, the grown-up supporting them can be reinforcing the learning point, 'Look! The bells are *in front of* the box now. Are the bells *on* the box?' etc. Tidy the instruments up at the end and praise the children.

Follow-up ideas:
- Look out for action rhymes and songs which include similar words e.g. 'The Dinosaur Hunt' (activity 6.5), 'In and out the dusty bluebells', 'When I was one I ate a bun' etc.
- Look out for natural opportunities to reinforce these concepts e.g. 'Please could you put an instrument *in front of* each child?' etc.

8. Concepts and understanding

Activity 8.7: The Music Man

Skill: To learn the words of the musical instruments
Target link: L3 L4 V6 A7
Early Learning Goal link: PS1 KW12 PD4 PD6 CD1

What to do:

Start by introducing the 'Music Man' song and actions which you will find in *Okki-tokki-unga*. Then try this variation.

Leader: 'I am the music man, I come from down your way,
and I can play ...'
Children: 'What can you play?'
Leader: 'I play the *triangle*.'

Now pick up a triangle, ask the children to repeat its name, and show them how you play it. Show how it makes a horrible sound if you hold the metal. Say how clever it is to dangle it by the string and what a good sound it makes if you then strike it. Let the children sing the chorus as you play the triangle.

Now repeat for other instruments, choosing three or four to demonstrate each time.

Follow-up ideas:
- You can use this activity as part of band time too, inviting just the tambourines to play for one verse, or just the drums for another, whilst you all sing the words.
- Provide an activity sheet with a picture of all your instruments and invite your children to colour in the different instruments they have played each session until gradually the sheet is all coloured; this is one way of encouraging the children to try different instruments and not always the same favourites.
- Sing 'We can play on the big bass drum' (*Okki-tokki-unga*).

Activity 8.8: This Old Man

Skill: To listen to and think of rhyming words
Target link: V1 V5 V6 M1 M5 S1 S8 A5
Early Learning Goal link: LL1 LL6 LL13 LL14

What to do:
Research has suggested that children who can hear rhymes in words and syllables may be less likely to have specific difficulties in reading letter sounds later on. Much of your rhyming and singing will be helping this skill. You can also adapt a familiar rhyming song by asking the children to fill in missing words.

This tune is likely to be familiar to you.

This old man, he played one,
He played nick-nack on my...

At this stage, stop and invite the children to think of a rhyming word to go with 'one'. They will find this very hard at first, so you might need to suggest pairs yourself until the children tell you that the two words sound the same; 'One...pot!, one....umbrella!, one...bun!' etc. Make it obvious for them. (If you get some silly or rude answers, do not flinch, but ask for another word instead!)

Finish each verse with the chorus:

With a nick-nack-paddywack, give a dog a bone,
This old man came rolling home.

Provide a repetitive action for any non-verbal children to join in during the chorus, a bounce on a knee, a clapping, or a rolling action. Continue with higher numbers, up to four or five.

Follow-up ideas:
- Look for other action rhymes which enable the children to think of their own words e.g. 'When I was one, I ate a bun'.
- You will find other activities to teach basic concepts such as high/low, up/down, loud/quiet, quick/slow in Chapters 7 and 9.

Chapter 9
Band time

Children find the musical instruments particularly motivating. Here are eight activities to encourage them to learn together as they enjoy joining in with their instruments. You will find a tape recorder and selection of tapes useful if you do not have access to live music.

Activity 9.1: Join the Band

Skill: To join in with musical instruments, starting and stopping when the leader does
Target link: G1 G2 G3 G4 L1 L3 L4 V2 V5 V6 A1 A7 I1 I2 I3 I5 I6 I8
Early Learning Goal link: LL1 PD6 CD1 CD8

What to do:
This is the best warm-up for band time. It is best to keep band time until the end of the session, say, the last ten minutes. This is because the children usually find this activity the most enjoyable, and they would be disappointed to have to put the instruments away and resume action songs afterwards. Instead, use it as the climax of your session. When children are particularly fretful or inattentive, you can move into band time sooner and have a shorter session, ending on a successful 'note'.

Put the musical instruments (see Chapter 3) in a box, and place it in the centre of the circle. Invite each child to come and choose an instrument for themselves. If you have more than ten children, you might like to name children to come forwards to choose so that everyone is not taking at once. Make sure children with particular needs also make a personal choice wherever possible; do not restrict them by selecting what you wish them to play. Make sure all the grown-ups have an instrument too.

Invite the children to watch you; 'When I play, you play too. When I stop, you stop too'. Put on your musical cassette or start to play your instrument. After a minute or so, stop, and look around the faces. Praise children by name for looking and listening. Repeat this three or four times, perhaps 'catching them out' with a very short passage at the end.

Follow-up idea:
- Move straight on to do up to two other band time activities within any one session.

The Music Makers Approach

Activity 9.2: Loudly and Quietly

Skill: To play an instrument loudly or quietly in imitation
Target link: G1 G2 G3 G4 L1 L3 L4 L7 V2 V5 V6 U9 A1 A7 I1 I2 I3 I5 I6 I8 I10
Early Learning Goal link: LL1 PD6 CD1 CD8

What to do:

Once the children are starting and stopping in a controlled and attentive way, introduce a new challenge. 'I wonder who can play their instrument very *quietly*?' Take up a percussion instrument yourself, and encourage everyone to play very quietly. Praise them for being so clever; it is *much* harder to play quietly than loudly.

Now challenge them to play as loudly as possible. Warn quieter children first and allow them to put hands over ears. With children who are very noise-sensitive, you are going to have to leave the really loud playing until they are more used to the group. Also, be conscious of any children with radio aids and hearing aids, taking care to avoid uncomfortable noises or volumes.

Now introduce the main activity: 'When you hear the music playing very *quietly*, see if you can play *quietly* too. When you hear it playing *loudly*, you play *loudly* too. You will have to *look* and to *listen* very carefully.' Play passages of music, each a minute or so long. Vary the loudness from two extremes; loud or very quiet. Praise the children by name, using the words you are teaching; 'Sultan, you *are* playing *quietly*' etc.

Follow-up ideas:
- Once the children are familiar with this activity, see if they can accompany a longer passage of music which starts quietly, gets gradually louder, then becomes quiet again.
- Introduce a hand-signal for loud (e.g. arms pushing upwards) and quiet (e.g. arms damping downwards), and invite a second grown-up or older child to conduct you all.

9. Band time

Activity 9.3: Runaway Train

Skill: To play an instrument fast or slow in imitation
Target link: G1 G2 G3 G4 L1 L3 L4 L8 V2 V5 V6 S8 A1 A7 I1 I2 I3 I5 I6 I7 I8 I9
Early Learning Goal link: LL1 PD6 CD1 CD8

What to do:
Introduce this activity in a similar way to 9.2. First, make sure the children understand how to play 'fast' and 'slow', then build it into an activity.

Tell the children you are going to play some train music. Let's pretend that the steam train has stopped in the station. 'Is everybody on board? Are all the doors closed? Here comes the guard, and she's going to blow her whistle! Count with me ... *one ... two ... three ...*' Give one of your helpers a whistle to blow.

The best music for this is the country dance tune 'Runaway train', played on a tuned instrument, though other train-like music would suit. Start very slowly, and provide a running commentary to the children; 'We're pulling out of the station ... getting faster ... very fast ... here comes a hill ... I think I can I think I can ... over the hill and fast again ... here comes a station ... slowing down ... slower ... all stop!' (etc.) Repeat the whistle blowing when you start off again, and repeat for two or three stations.

If you prefer, you can play this activity without music. Make sure you have a few adults or older children to provide a strong beat, taking their lead from your own percussion instrument. Include a strong drum, scratchy sounds, and shaking sounds to give the impression of a train in motion.

Follow-up ideas:
- Sit in a long line and pretend you are the carriages.
- Invite different children to be the guard and blow the whistle, particularly if you have a child who is practising blowing sounds in their speech and language therapy. Use an antiseptic wipe for hygiene if you are passing the whistle between children.

The Music Makers Approach

Activity 9.4: Musical Swaps

Skill: To encourage children to try a range of different percussion instruments
Target link: G1 G2 G3 G4 L1 L3 L4 V2 V5 V6 A1 A7 I1 I2 I3 I5 I6 I8
Early Learning Goal link: LL1 PD6 CD1 CD8

What to do:

Repeat activity 9.1, and each time the music stops, encourage the children to try a different instrument. Pause whilst the grown-ups check that each child knows how to play their choice, ensuring that triangles are held in a position for the best sound, that hand drums are beaten with hands and snare drums with beaters, that cymbals do not catch noses, that indian bells are moved up and down against each other and not struck like cymbals etc.

You may have children who need to practise certain actions, perhaps following a programme from the physiotherapist or occupational therapist; parents can keep you informed. They might need to practise shaking, handling two objects at once, striking one object with another, or bringing a weak hand into use. Think about this creatively so that you can encourage the playing of instruments which are going to teach these skills.

Repeat for three or four instruments.

Follow-up ideas:
- Build this activity into the 'Music Man' song (activity 8.7).
- Use the activity sheet suggested in 8.7.

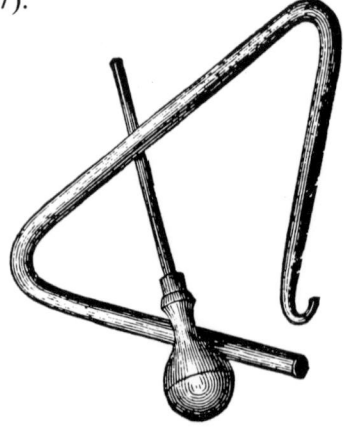

9. Band time

Activity 9.5: Leading the Band

Skill: To become confident enough to start and stop the whole band
Target link: G1 G2 G3 G4 L1 L3 L4 V2 V5 V6 A1 A7 I1 I2 I3 I5 I6 I8 I11
Early Learning Goal link: PS1 LL1 PD6 CD1 CD8

What to do:

Once the children are used to activity 9.1, exchange your role with one of the children. When they start to play, everyone starts to play. When they stop, everyone does. Have a supporting grown-up sitting alongside that child to encourage and prompt if needed.

This works very well for children who have very little confidence, but is best done after four or five music sessions, when they are feeling secure. It also works well for the contrary child. Occasionally, one child starts to play as you stop and stops as you start! This is best tackled by ignoring, at the same time praising by name the children who are co-operating with the aim of the activity. However, you can be pleasantly surprised if you then 'turn the tables', copying the starting and stopping of this child. Suddenly, you are all giving positive attention and the child is joining the new activity appropriately without even setting out to! There may be an initial crossness, then a big smile and a sense of pride in the influence (s)he is having on all the others.

This activity is also excellent for children with autistic or communication difficulties. They may not have found the action rhymes motivating, but are likely to enjoy the instruments. By encouraging the others to start playing when a certain child does and to stop when they do, you can sometimes see the point where a child 'in a world of his/her own' suddenly notes with delight that the whole group is mirroring them. You can then encourage several 'turn-takes' of playing as you copy and respond together.

Follow-up ideas:
- Allow different children to lead the march, again starting and stopping the entire proceedings.
- Give a child a drum to beat or a whistle to blow to signal 'start' and 'stop'.

The Music Makers Approach

Activity 9.6: Musical Stories

Skill: To select sound effects for a familiar story
Learning Goal link: L1 L6 A1 A2 I1 I2 I3 I4 I5 I6
Early Learning Goal link: PS4 LL1 LL5 PD6 CD1 CD4 CD8 CD11

What to do:

Choose a short story that the children are already very familiar with e.g. 'Billy Goats Gruff' or 'Three Little Pigs'. Remind the children of the main storyline. Now invite them to choose some sounds to go with the story.

Place a selection of instruments in the centre of the circle, including other sources of sound effects e.g. crinkly paper, a washboard and wooden spoon, a thunder sheet, coconut shells, blowing tubes, steam train whistle etc.

Go over the story and encourage a discussion and experimentation so that the group can select the best sounds to go with the story. Make sure every child is included. Use a grown-up helper to prompt the children and encourage them to come in at the right time. Rehearse the whole story together, and then tell it to the parents and carers at home time.

Follow-up ideas:
- Invite all the children to select instruments to make 'happy' music, 'cross' music, 'scary' music, 'sleepy' music etc.
- Look for opportunities for the children to use the musical instruments creatively and combine them in new and interesting ways. Always make sure each and every child has a role to play, even if they find it hard to think creatively themselves.

9. Band time

Activity 9.7: Watch the Conductor

Skill: To look and respond to a hand signal
Target link: G1 G2 G3 G4 L1 L3 L4 V2 V5 V6 A1 A7 I1 I2 I3 I5 I6 I8
Early Learning Goal link: LL1 PD6 CD1 CD8

What to do:

This is an activity for children well used to the routines of the music session, and well used to both looking and listening. In this activity, you choose the instruments which you would like the children to play. Give them out in sections so that all the children with shakers are next to each other, then the drums, then the jingle bells etc.

Tell the children that they will need to watch very carefully, because the conductor will show them when to start and when to stop. Introduce the two hand signals; a downwards arm movement for 'start' and a policeman's halt signal for 'stop'.

You can either be the conductor yourself, in which case you will need a helper to operate the tape or to play the accompaniment. Alternatively, you provide the music but use a helper to conduct. Practise starting and stopping to the conductor's signal.

Now tell the children that the conductor will point to different groups of instruments and tell them when to start and stop. Start the tape or accompaniment, and ask the conductor to signal to the drums, to the bells, to the shakers etc., when they are to join in and when they are to stop. Start by bringing the groups of instruments in gradually, have a central section with everyone taking part, then gradually fade the music as different sections drop out again. Praise the children for looking.

Follow-up ideas:
- This makes a good display for an open day or concert. Keep it relaxed and happy. Introduce other hand signals too to make this more challenging, e.g. 'start', 'stop', 'loud', 'soft'.

The Music Makers Approach

Activity 9.8: Marching

Skill: To develop a one-two rhythm, and to move whilst playing an instrument
Target link: G1 G2 G4 L3 L4 L6 V6 M1 M2 M4 M5 M6 U9 I1 I2 I3 I4 I5 I6 I8 I12
Early Learning Goal link: PS1 LL1 PD1 PD6 CD1 CD4 CD8

What to do:

Once children are confident within the sessions, this is a good activity to finish on.

Invite the children to choose an instrument they can carry, and to line up behind you. This should be voluntary, and children who prefer to can remain in the circle, contributing to the background music. Make sure that children who are non-ambulant have a chance to be wheeled or carried in the march if they want to.

Move around the outside of the circle, playing your own instrument as you go (or ask one of your helpers to work the tape). Encourage the children to march behind you, playing their instruments as they go. Stamp your feet, and have a strong drum beat, to emphasise the strong one-two rhythm of the march. Children learn rhythms best if they can move to them.

Every now and then, stop the music and turn round to see who is following you. Praise children by name for looking and listening well. Do not expect the little ones to stay in line; you are likely to find a rather general meandering and this is perfectly acceptable. If you have the opportunity, prepare spaces ahead so that you can all move into other areas of the pre-school, or even outdoors if appropriate.

Follow-up ideas:
- Allow other children to lead the march from time to time.
- Use a march as part of your summer fete or Christmas party, to show off to the parents.
- Look for ways of making your instruments portable, e.g. drums on straps which should go over a shoulder for safety.

Resource list
References

In this chapter, there is an example of how the Music Makers Approach was used to encourage children who had SEN to make progress within their local playgroup. You will be given a 'snapshot' of a setting so that you can visualise what a typical music session might look like.

Snapshot of Richie

First Music Makers session at a large 100-place town playgroup, with children in two large pre-fabricated huts according to their age. I am given the three-to-four-year-olds; about 30 of them with four adults who do not look very confident with the proceedings.

Richie is running around, shouting and jumping off the tables. He has recently been diagnosed as having Asperger's Syndrome. His parents are understandably upset and extremely tense. Perhaps partly for this reason, Richie's behaviour has almost been beyond control during the last few days. It is his father who has brought him today.

I start with a warm-up song. The children look happy and watch carefully. The adults still look unsure and do not sing. Richie is held on his Dad's knee and immediately goes into full struggle and scream, beating his father and shouting 'silly music'. We battle on. He escapes. I explain to his father that I would like to see him go his own way to see if I can attract him with the music. Dad tells me 'You'll be lucky'. We try again. The children are joining in with a clapping song, and the adults 'unfreezing'.

We sing the greeting song. Richie stops at his name and looks at me, smiling. He runs off again. We sing a wobbly jelly song. The children are now attending beautifully, with the exception of Richie. Merle has severe speech and language delay and is watching attentively, joining in the actions. Ben 'never sits still' and has attention difficulties; he is watching me closely and following the clues.

I lay the percussion instruments out on the floor, asking the children to wait until I have finished before choosing, and (just as I am about to invite Richie to choose first), Richie darts in and grabs a drum and a stick. He takes it to a side table away from the group and is absorbed in beating it. We all play; I tell the children to play when I play and stop when I stop. We have a few goes. They all look and listen for my piano accordion attentively, even those with listening difficulties.

I then explain we will start when Richie starts and stop when Richie stops. After two goes of this, Richie looks up at me with a full and almost startling eye contact. He drums furiously and stops. We all join in loudly. He smiles. He gives one soft tap. We copy. He plays a long string. We copy. By this time, he is grinning and I feel in full reciprocal communication with him. He looks playful for a moment as he sees just how quiet he can be and we still hear him and copy. This carries on for a full four minutes. Richie is leading the band. Dad is smiling.

We start to march around Richie and his drum. When I halt, everyone stops, and we do not start until Richie beats his drum again. This takes us to the end of the 20 minutes. Richie occasionally 'runs off some steam', but then returns to his drum.

Chapter 11
The evaluative research

This chapter briefly describes an evaluation of the Music Makers Approach, based on the Action Research model. The aim of the original Music Makers project was to develop reflective practice in early years educators and to enable them to improve the developmental skills of any children who have SEN in their settings.

Fifty-four early years educators attached to 29 settings were trained in the approach and used the methods they had learned to target 49 children with SEN. Questionnaire data were collected to evaluate how early years educators were developing their practice following training. The developmental checklist shown on page 73 was designed, its reliability between observers checked, and used to measure changes in the children's skills. Thirty early years educators were interviewed six months after training and the transcripts analysed using 'content analysis' and 'Grounded Theory'.

All settings continued to use the Music Makers Approach 12 months after training. It was seen by them as increasing both their own and the children's confidence and encouraging all the children to join in. Many reflected on the positive changes they had seen in all the children's motivation, behaviour and confidence and how this was also generalising to other learning situations.

There were 49 children each with very individual special educational needs and each attending very different settings with very different people. Inevitably, their rates of progress were individual and unique. Nevertheless, early years educators were left with the overwhelming impression that they had all made good progress across each area of the checklist (page 73). Progress was dependent on early years educators selecting appropriate activities to meet individual needs, and many of them felt more able to do this since using the Music Makers Approach.

The reasons early years educators gave for the children's progress were varied and again suggested much reflective thought about the effect they could have upon their children's learning. Many considered that progress was linked to the children's enjoyment of the music sessions, their better ability to look and to listen in this kind of approach, their response to the familiar routine, and their increased confidence.

The following theoretical model describing the relationships which exist when adults and children learn together began to emerge. When early years educators reflect carefully about their practice, they become better able to meet the individual needs of the children they are working with. This, in turn, enables them to see evidence of the children's progress and contribute further to encouraging and maintaining it. The more the children progress, the greater the confidence of the educator, and the more individually they become able to meet needs. The progress of the one affects the progress of the other as adult and child learn together.

Young children respond well to set structures and routines which enable them to anticipate and predict. This, in turn, seems to improve their confidence as learners, their ability to attend and their motivation to join in. With familiarity comes better attention, more appropriate behaviour, and more opportunities to learn.

11. The evaluative research

However, set structures and routines also help the early years educator to develop her or his own skills and confidence, making them better able to deliver the curriculum with that level of flexibility and creativity needed to ensure that individual needs are met, moment by moment. Learning in both adults and children is therefore an ongoing process.

Practical 'how to do it' approaches enable early years educators to develop their skills and confidence. If such approaches 'work' in the sense that the children respond positively and make progress, then those approaches tend to be used long after the training period has ended. This enables further practice and development of skills which can then be generalised to new learning situations. It also allows any belief systems which have been strengthened by the approach (e.g. that 'inclusion works') to take root. Finally, it also allows the early years educator to develop the skills and confidence needed to help the children generalise their progress to new situations.

With practice and confidence comes the ability of early years educators to develop new teaching styles and approaches. They become able to 'take risks' in leaving their regular routines in order to 'go with the child', the opportunity and the moment. In fact, they have developed the ability to think reflectively about what it is they can do to enhance the children's learning and plan their next approaches in light of this, not only in their planning but 'on the hoof' as well.

The Music Makers Approach has been successful in encouraging pre-school workers to think reflectively about their practice and to develop their approaches so as best to enhance the children's learning and progress. This is despite many of them having little previous experience or training. The success of the approach may be because it supports the interaction between adults and children, developing the skills and confidences of both and enabling the success of one to foster the success of the other. It may also be because it allows the learning process to be extended over time and leads to generalisation of skills from one area to another. Settings tend to continue to use the approach independently long after their training is completed.

It has also been shown to improve the developmental skills of children who have SEN, again perhaps because it uses routines and builds confidence over time. However, early years educators have found it to be an approach for all children (not just those with SEN), and it has therefore proved to be a practical way of delivering the early years curriculum inclusively.

Early Learning Goals
Reference numbers used in activity sheets

By the end of the foundation stage, most children will:

Personal, Social and Emotional Development

PS1	be confident to try new activities, initiate ideas and speak in a familiar group
PS2	form good relationships with peers
PS3	form good relationships with adults
PS4	work as part of a group or class
PS5	maintain attention, concentrate, and sit quietly when appropriate
PS7/8	continue to be interested, excited and motivated to learn
PS9	select and use activities and resources independently
PS10	dress and undress independently and manage their own personal hygiene
PS11/17	have a developing awareness of their own needs, views and feelings and be sensitive to the needs, views and feelings of others
PS12	understand that people have different needs, views, cultures and beliefs, which need to be treated with respect
PS13	take turns and share fairly, understanding that there needs to be agreed values and codes of behaviour for groups, including adults and children, to work together harmoniously
PS14/19	respond to significant experiences, showing a range of feelings when appropriate
PS15	consider the consequences of their words and actions for themselves and others
PS16	understand what is right, what is wrong, and why
PS18	have a developing respect for their own cultures and beliefs and those of other people, and understand that they can expect others to treat their needs, views, cultures and beliefs with respect

Also covered:
PS6   they are able to seek help where needed

Language and Literacy

LL1	enjoy listening to and using spoken and written language, and readily turn to it in their play and learning, and sustain attentive listening, responding to what they have heard by relevant comments, questions or actions
LL2	use talk to organise, sequence and clarify thinking, ideas, feelings and events
LL3	extend their vocabulary, exploring the meanings and sounds of new words
LL4	interact with others, negotiating plans and activities and taking turns in conversation, and speak clearly and audibly with confidence and control and show awareness of the listener, for example through their use of conventions such as greetings, 'please' and 'thank you'
LL5/6/7	listen with enjoyment and respond to stories, songs and other music, rhymes and poems and make up their own stories, songs, rhymes and poems, and retell narratives in the correct sequence, drawing on the language patterns of stories
LL8	use language to imagine and recreate roles and experiences
LL10	show an understanding of the elements of stories, such as main characters, sequence of events, and openings, and how information can be found in non-fiction texts to answer questions about where, who, why and how

Reference numbers used in activity sheets

LL11/12	know that print carries meaning and, in English, is read from left to right and top to bottom
LL13	explore and experiment with sounds, words and texts, and hear and say initial and final sounds in words, and short vowel sounds within words
LL14/17	link sounds to letters, naming and sounding the letters of the alphabet
LL15/16	read a range of familiar and common words and simple sentences independently
LL18	use a pencil and hold it effectively to form recognisable letters, most of which are correctly formed
LL19	use their phonic knowledge to write simple regular words and make phonetically plausible attempts at more complex words
LL20	attempt writing for various purposes, using features of different forms such as lists, stories and instructions
LL21	write their own names and other things such as labels and captions and begin to form simple sentences, sometimes using punctuation

Also covered:

LL9	children enjoy books and handle them carefully

Mathematics

M1	use language such as 'circle' or 'bigger' to describe the shape and size of solids and flat shapes
M2	use everyday words to describe position, and use language such as 'more' or 'less', 'greater' or 'smaller', 'heavier' or 'lighter', to compare two numbers or quantities
M3	talk about, recognise, and recreate simple patterns
M4	in practical activities and discussion begin to use the vocabulary involved in adding and subtracting
M5	say and use number names in order in familiar contexts
M6/7	count reliably up to ten everyday objects
M8	recognise numerals 1 to 9
M9	find one more or one less than a number from 1 to 10
M10	use developing mathematical ideas and methods to solve practical problems
M11/12	begin to relate addition to combining two groups of objects, and subtraction to 'taking away'

Knowledge and Understanding of the World

KW1	find out about their environment, and talk about those features they like and dislike
KW2/3	find out about past and present events in their own lives, and in those of their families and other people they know
KW4/6	observe, find out about, and identify features in the place they live and the natural world
KW5	find out about, and identify some features of, living things, objects and events they observe
KW7	look closely at similarities, differences, patterns and change
KW8/9	investigate objects and materials by using all of their senses as appropriate
KW10/11	ask questions about why things happen and how things work

KW12	build and construct with a wide range of objects, selecting appropriate resources, and adapting their work where necessary
KW13	select the tools and techniques they need to shape, assemble and join the materials they are using
KW14	find out about and identify the uses of everyday technology, and use information and communication technology and programmable toys to support their learning
PS12/18	begin to know about their own cultures and beliefs and those of other people

Physical Development

PD1	move with confidence, imagination and in safety
PD2	move with control and co-ordination
PD3	show awareness of space, of themselves and of others
PD4	use a range of small and large equipment
PD5	travel around, under, over and through balancing and climbing equipment
PD6/7	handle tools, objects, construction and malleable materials safely and with increasing control
PD8	recognise the importance of keeping healthy and those things which contribute to this
PD9	recognise the changes that happen to their bodies when they are active

Creative Development

CD1	recognise and explore how sounds can be changed, sing simple songs from memory, recognise repeated sounds and sound patterns and match movements to music
CD2	explore colour, texture, shape, form and space in two and three dimensions
CD3	respond in a variety of ways to what they see
CD4	respond in a variety of ways to what they hear
CD5	respond in a variety of ways to what they smell
CD6	respond in a variety of ways to what they touch and feel
CD7	use their imagination in art and design
CD8	also in music
CD9	also in dance
CD10	also in stories and imaginative and role play
CD11/12	express and communicate their ideas, thoughts and feelings by using a widening range of materials, suitable tools, imaginative and role play, movement, designing and making, and a variety of songs and musical instruments

Music Makers
Assessment and record-keeping sheet

Name of Child: _____ **Date:** _____

Name of Adult completing this assessment _____ **Setting:** _____

In the Initial Assessment column:
  please enter one tick if (s)he can do that skill just sometimes
    and two ticks if (s)he can do that skill almost always

In the Target Skill column:
  please tick skills you would really like her/him to learn in the music group during the next term

Activity	Date	Initial Assessment	Target Skill	Final Assessment

G: GENERAL
1. Stops fretting during music
2. Enjoys music
3. Joins in group on parent's knee
4. Begins to join in independently

L: LISTENING
1. Turns towards a sound
2. Recognises familiar TV tunes
3. Starts playing when leader does
4. Stops playing when leader does
5. Finds familiar sound from choice of two
6. Imitates simple rhythm with prompt
7. Plays loudly/quietly in imitation
8. Plays quickly/slowly in imitation

V: LOOKING
1. Turns to look at person singing
2. Turns from one sound to another
3. Gives eye contact when greeted
4. Looks towards a hidden sound
5. Watches other children
6. Looks at group leader occasionally

M: MOVEMENT
1. Allows self to be bounced on knee
2. Makes general movements to music
3. Allows arms to be moved to music
4. Allows legs to be moved to music
5. Bounces when held in standing position
6. Dances/moves independently to music
7. Moves fast/slow to different music

The Music Makers Approach

Activity	Initial Assessment Date	Target Skill	Final Assessment

S: SINGING AND VOCALISING
1. Makes general sounds to music
2. Makes 'tuneful' sounds to music
3. Tries to sing familiar songs
4. Joins in animal sounds
5. Joins in repeated sounds b-b etc.
6. Joins in key words e.g. 'down'
7. Says familiar phrases e.g. 'e-i-e-i-o'
8. Counts to three

U: UNDERSTANDING
1. Turns to his/her name
2. Points to one or two body parts
3. Points to several body parts
4. Responds to up/down
5. Responds to high/low
6. Responds to loud/quiet
7. Points to some named colours
8. 'Shows me' five fingers
9. Responds to 'look', 'listen'

A: ACTIONS
1. Allows self to be prompted
2. Demonstrates awareness of what comes next
3. Claps hands to request
4. Waves 'bye bye' in imitation
5. Joins in clapping song
6. Moves hands for high/low
7. Copies new actions

I: INSTRUMENTS
1. Holds shaking instrument when placed in hand
2. Can shake instrument
3. Copies a hand beat on tambourine
4. Holds two things at once
5. Beats two parts of instrument together
6. Beats drum with stick
7. Blows instrument
8. Joins in the band
9. Plays fast/slow to different music
10. Plays quiet/loud to different music
11. Leads the band
12. Marches and plays at same time

Music Makers
Session planning sneet

	Date	Target ref.	ELG ref.

Warm-up:
(Chapters 4 and 5)

Greeting song:
(Chapter 4)

Action rhyme(s):
(Chapters 5 and 8)

Looking and listening game:
(Chapter 6)

Movement:
(Chapter 7)

Spoken rhyme:
(Chapters 5, 6, 7, 8)

Band time:
(Chapter 9)

Goodbye song:
(Chapter 4)

Resource list and references

References

DfE (1994) *Code of Practice on the Identification and Assessment of Special Educational Needs.* Suffolk: DfEE Publications.

QCA and DfEE (2000) *Curriculum Guidance for the Foundation Stage.* Hayes: QCA Publications.

Song books

Harrop, B., Friend, L. and Gadsby, D. (1975) *Okki-tokki-unga: Action Songs for Children.* London: A & C Black.

Pavelko, V. and Scott, L.B. (1976) *Apusskidu: Songs for Children.* London: A & C Black.

Hayes, S. and Goffe, T. (1988) *Stamp your Feet.* London: Walker Books.

Useful catalogues

Early Learning Centre (for tapes, instruments and song books): contact your local branch, or telephone Head Office on: 01793 831300.

SBS (Step by Step) (for colourful and more unusual musical instruments suitable for early years and SEN): Holgate Street, Waterhead, Oldham, Lancs. OL4 2JF (Tel. 0845 300 1089).

NES Arnold Ltd (for musical instruments and props): Ludlow Hill Road, West Bridgford, Nottingham NG2 6HD (Tel. 0115 971 7700).

LDA (e.g. audio tapes for listening activities): Duke Street, Wisbech, Cambs. PE13 2AE (Tel: 01223 365445).

Philip and Tacey's Language 2000 (e.g. audio tapes for listening activities): North Way, Andover, Hampshire SP10 5BA (Tel: 01264 332171).

For information on Portage Training

Contact: National Portage Association, 127 Monks Dale, Yeovil BA21 3JE.